Breaking Free

Breaking Free

Bible studies on the **liberating** call of Jesus

Mark William Olson

Judson Press
Valley Forge

Breaking Free

Bible Studies on the Liberating Call of Jesus

Illustrations by Cathleen Benberg.

Judson Press has made every effort to trace the ownership of all quotes. In the event of a question arising from the use of a quote, we regret any error made and will be pleased to make the necessary correction in future printings and editions of this book.

Unless otherwise indicated, Bible quotations in this volume are from The Holy Bible, King James Version. Bible quotations marked (NRSV) are from the New Revised Standard Version of the Bible, copyright © 1989 by the Division of Christian Education of the National Council of the Churches of Christ in the United States of America. Used by permission. All rights reserved. Bible quotations marked (NJB) are from The New Jerusalem Bible, copyright © 1985 by Darton, Longman & Todd, Ltd. and Doubleday, a division of Random House, Inc. Reprinted by permission.

Library of Congress Cataloging-in-Publication Data

Olson, Mark William.
    Breaking free : Bible studies on the liberating call of Jesus / Mark William Olson.
        p. cm.
    Includes bibliographic references.
    ISBN 0-8170-1409-8 (pbk. : alk. paper)
    1. Bible. N.T. Mark—Study and teaching. I. Title.

BS2585.55 O57 2001
226.3'0071'5—dc21
    2001041411

CONTENTS

INTRODUCTION

WELCOME

This book is designed for individual or group Bible study. It focuses on the liberating call of Jesus, especially as it is found in the Gospel of Mark. Break free and follow—that's what Jesus calls us to do.

If you don't already love the Gospel of Mark and the powerful message it contains, I hope you will find yourself thoroughly in love with this Gospel by the time you finish working your way through these easy-to-use study sessions—with an appetite whetted for more.

As you will discover, no other portion of Scripture enters more closely or more purely into the heart of the Christian message than does this remarkable Gospel. Not only is Mark one of the earliest biblical portrayals of Jesus, but also it is among the most dramatic and captivating books in all of Scripture. It is a profound and compelling book of theology, carefully crafted by a master storyteller who interweaves scene after scene with so many surprising and dramatic twists that we almost can't bear to leave it.

With narrative power, the unknown author of this Gospel presents his understanding of who Jesus is and his even deeper understanding of who God is. The Gospel of Mark is filled with allusions to earlier Jewish Scriptures. Again and again, the author connects his message with the work of Jewish psalmists and prophets who have gone before.

Every scene bristles with passion—not just because the author is a great storyteller but also because the author is deeply committed to personal transformation: our transformation. He wants to introduce us to God and to God's great ways. He longs for those ways to become our ways so that we might face the challenges of our world with courage and faith.

On one level, Jesus is the center of the story. But the Gospel of Mark sees the story of Jesus as the tip of the iceberg. This is not a dry, historical account of one man's conflict with the Roman authorities. It's not an academic biography. And it's not meant to be understood as a verbatim transcript of everything that one man from Nazareth said and did.

This Gospel is much broader than that. It deals in cosmic proportions. It rises way above the everyday details that are so vividly sketched out. This is a Gospel about the heavens opening. This is a Gospel about a bully being brought low. This is a Gospel about the power and compassion of God—for all humanity, for all people, in every situation. This is a Gospel that invites each of us to break free and follow, a Gospel that invites each of us to take up our beds and walk.

As you work your way through these Bible studies, you'll find yourself looking at more than Mark. Each session includes important passages from other portions of Scripture, passages that the Jewish author of this Gospel seems to be deliberately building on or alluding to.

In the end, you'll gain a deeper appreciation for the liberating call of Jesus in your life and a deeper appreciation for the ways in which the call of Jesus has always been rooted in and connected to the dynamic Jewish faith of which he was a part.

So open your heart. Open your mind. Open your soul. Plunge into these studies, for there's a call in the air, a call that sometimes comes when we least expect it. This call may also come when we most desire it. The God you will discover here is not a God of limitation but a God of liberation. Not a God of entrapment but a God of empowerment. Not a God of death but a God of life. Not a God of guilt but a God of grace.

To all who are oppressed, held back, or shut out, the rabbi from Nazareth whispers. Break free, he says. Break free and follow. Follow in God's way. Follow in freedom and hope. Follow in mercy and love.

Jesus' message is the message for us all: In breaking free from all that would hold us back, we can walk anew in the liberating ways of God.

HOW TO USE THESE STUDY SESSIONS

In this book you'll find enough material for fifteen in-depth study sessions, or as many as twenty-one sessions if you divide the longer ones in half. These lessons were developed and refined at Shiloh Baptist Church (Old Site) in Fredericksburg, Virginia, where a wonderfully open group of people met weekly in an effort to unlock the meaning and power of this Gospel for themselves.

The group was committed to the idea that no one other than the weekly discussion leader would read or study the background material in advance. This made it easier for newcomers to visit. Everyone was always at the same starting point. Likewise, everyone could discuss the biblical texts and the included commentaries with an equal degree of freshness. Everyone advanced at the same pace, which helped build community and fostered a sense of equality and trust.

The pattern that evolved for the original group was to sit together in a large circle. We took turns reading aloud each portion of each session, as we felt led. That's why the comments on some biblical texts are broken into several smaller units. It gets boring and burdensome (and sometimes intimidating) if one person reads aloud too long. So each session's commentaries are divided into small, manageable units.

As a group, we all looked up in our Bibles each biblical text that we came to. Whoever felt so led would read the text aloud for the group. When we came to discussion questions, we paused to consider the questions raised. But we never called on anyone for an answer. People entered into discussion as they felt comfortable. In addition, as we went along, we made sure that all present felt free to share their insights, questions, thoughts, and personal experiences whenever they felt like it. Using this method developed a good group spirit.

We aimed to keep each session to an hour. But often, when the discussions got particularly lively or when the group's own questions got extensive, folks sometimes chose to keep going a bit longer. We decided to meet on a day and at a time when most participants had somewhat flexible schedules. This gave us a real advantage in probing the Gospel message in depth. If your group has less time or is bound by fixed schedules, you might want to shorten some of the sessions or divide a few of them in half. Suggestions for those with limited time appear where appropriate.

When we first used this material, we found that not everyone was able to be present every week. And we didn't expect everyone to be. Because each session begins with a review of the immediate biblical context ("Setting the Stage"), you should find that variations in attendance patterns aren't a problem. And because no homework or advance preparation is required, no one ever needs to feel out of it.

Most of those in our group used the King James Version of the Scriptures. Because that version sticks rather literally to the Greek text of Mark, it isn't a bad version to use when studying this Gospel. The Revised Standard Version or New Revised Standard Version would be suitable as well.

However, when studying this Gospel, it's best to avoid casual para-phrases and interpretive translations, including the Living or Amplified Bibles, which tend to insert their own somewhat misleading explanations into the text. In the end, such interpretive versions can do more harm than good, especially in a group Bible study, for they can obscure or dis-tort Mark's carefully crafted message.

You may have previously participated in Bible studies that jump from one Gospel to another. You'll find none of that here. This is an effort to look intensively at the liberating call of Jesus in one Gospel, the Gospel of Mark, a book that was written to be read and understood on its own. So as a group, we deliberately avoided comparing the accounts in Mark with the accounts in any of the other Gospels, all of which were written some-time after Mark. Looking at other Gospels would only dilute the integrity and intentionality of Mark's unique perspective. So we didn't do it.

Likewise, you should know that this study makes no effort to use the Gospel as a tool to uncover the historical Jesus. Those who develop elab-orate theories about which words in which Gospel reflect the verbatim words of Jesus and which deviate in some way from historical fact miss the point. Mark isn't history. Nor is it biography. Yes, there is a real person behind the story. But Mark is primarily a beautifully crafted, pow-erfully presented theology. To understand the enduring truth of its mes-sage—and to feel its deep challenge to our lives—we need to preserve its literary and dramatic integrity.

Each of the study sessions in this volume includes allusions to one or more hymns, gospel songs, or spirituals. Depending on the skills and in-clinations of your group, you may or may not want to join together in some singing. Or perhaps someone can provide a CD or other recording of the appropriate song to have playing as the group arrives. Music and art are included in each session because they, like the Gospel itself, are able to touch our emotions and reach deep into the innermost part of our souls.

Whether you study Mark on your own or with a group, we hope that you will find it as liberating and empowering as we have. Keep your mind open. Keep your heart open. The liberating call of Jesus is message that will change you. It's a message to knock loose your fears. A message to fill you with faith and hope. A message to return to again and again, for each time a new burden or obstacle has been thrown in our path, we need to hear once more the message of Jesus, inviting each of us to break free and follow . . .

THANKS

These Bible studies grew out of a group effort. And so, in writing the text for this volume, I am deeply indebted to the wonderful group of fellow pilgrims who undertook with me a lengthy study of Jesus' call in the Gospel of Mark. Their spiritual depth, personal maturity, and straightforward honesty in grappling with the issues that we encountered significantly broadened my own understanding of this important and life-changing Gospel.

Among those who have participated with me in the Bible study group out of which this material comes are Patricia Buckner, Norma Burruss, Mary Bridgewater, Maynard Clipper, Ethel Conway, Harold Conway, Daisy Conyers, Willie Conyers, Carrie Crump, Janice Davies, Jean Johnson, Althea Lucas, Reginald Lucas, Edyth McLaurine, Laura Montgomery, Robert Montgomery, Maxine Newell, Lillian Pryde, Verline Shepherd, Lynn Twyner, Lena Watson, and James Watson. I am grateful to all who played a role.

The wonderful fabric paintings included with each session were created especially for this book by my friend and work associate at A Distant Wind, Cathleen Benberg.

During the course of our group's original study, important information and insights were drawn from a variety of published sources. Although each of these books is different from the others and although some of the authors would find themselves in major disagreement with each other on some questions, we found all of these resources valuable in one way or another. They include, in alphabetical order by author:

G. R. Beasley-Murray, *Jesus and the Kingdom of God* (Grand Rapids, Mich.: Eerdmans, 1986).

Robert Beck, *Nonviolent Story: Narrative Conflict Resolution in the Gospel of Mark* (Maryknoll, N.Y.: Orbis, 1996).

Bruce Chilton, *Pure Kingdom: Jesus' Vision of God* (Grand Rapids, Mich.: Eerdmans, 1996).

Stevan L. Davies, *Jesus the Healer: Possession, Trance, and the Origins of Christianity* (New York: Continuum, 1995).

David Emmanuel Goatley, *Were You There? Godforsakenness in Slave Religion* (Maryknoll, N.Y.: Orbis, 1996).

Robert H. Gundry, *Mark: A Commentary on His Apology for the Cross* (Grand Rapids, Mich.: Eerdmans, 1993).

Robert G. Hamerton-Kelly, *The Gospel and the Sacred: Poetics of Violence in Mark* (Minneapolis: Fortress, 1994).

Jack Dean Kingsbury, *Conflict in Mark: Jesus, Authorities, Disciples* (Minneapolis: Fortress, 1989).

William L. Lane, *The Gospel According to Mark* (Grand Rapids, Mich.: Eerdmans, 1974).

Joel Marcus, *The Way of the Lord: Christological Exegesis of the Old Testament in the Gospel of Mark* (Louisville, Ky.: Westminster/John Knox, 1992).

Ched Myers, *Binding the Strong Man: A Political Reading of Mark's Story of Jesus* (Maryknoll, N.Y.: Orbis, 1988).

Mary Ann Tolbert, *Sowing the Gospel: Mark's World in Literary-Historical Perspective* (Minneapolis: Fortress, 1996).

Thanks are also due to the Reverend Lawrence A. Davies, the pastor of the church where this material came to life. His spiritual dedication, prayerful passion, powerful preaching, and compassionate insight have blessed and informed all of our understandings. We're grateful.

—*Mark William Olson*

SESSION 1

AND IMMEDIATELY
HE AROSE, TOOK
UP THE BED, AND
WENT FORTH BEFORE
THEM ALL . . .
—MARK 2:12

ANY BALM IN GILEAD?

MARK 2:1-15

Group leaders: This session runs slightly longer than most because it begins with some important background for this series of Bible studies. It's good to look at this material together, if you can, so that everyone is equally informed. This will also give you a chance to discuss any questions or insights that people might have. However, if you are operating under tight time constraints, you could break this session in half. One place to do that is just before reading Mark 2:6. Another option is to ask someone to summarize "Setting the Stage" for the group.

SETTING THE STAGE

PART ONE: The theme for this series of Bible studies is illustrated by a passage from the Book of Proverbs: "Break free like a gazelle from the trap, like a bird from the fowler's clutches" (Proverbs 6:5, NJB).

At times all of us can feel trapped, caught in a tight place with no way out. Sometimes we feel trapped by the oppressive actions of others. Sometimes we feel trapped by systems and structures beyond our control. Sometimes we feel trapped by our fears and insecurities. And sometimes we have made bad choices but don't know how to work ourselves free from the mess we've gotten ourselves in.

But as we will see through these Bible studies, the God of Scripture is not a God of entrapment but a God of empowerment. The God of Scripture is not a God of limitation but a God of liberation. The God of Scripture is not a God who holds us back but a God who sets us free.

When we are trapped in "the fowler's clutches," we lose the power to run in God's way. When we are trapped in "the fowler's clutches," the ways of sin and death and evil hold sway over our lives. That's why Proverbs calls on God's people to "break free like a gazelle." We are meant to run—meant to run with our Maker—for the sake of freedom, love, and mercy. We are meant to run in the ways of peace and life and hope.

To run like a gazelle, we can't be content with entrapment. To run like a gazelle, we have to dig deep within to find God's Spirit. To run like a gazelle, we have to throw off that which holds us back. We have to become actors in our own cause, not just those who are cruelly acted upon. Hearing God's call and remembering who made us, we have to take action. We have to say, "I'll be bound no more! No more chains holding me!"

PART TWO: In the chapters that follow, we'll look together at the liberating call of Jesus as it is presented in the Gospel of Mark, which is widely believed to be the oldest of the biblical Gospels. Like all of the Gospels, Mark presents a powerful and compelling portrait of Jesus and his liberating interactions with people around him—people like us, people struggling to break free, struggling to escape the traps and burdens that are forever thrown in our path.

As we look together at Mark, we'll discover people learning from Jesus in at least three ways. One way they learn is through his preaching. We're told that Jesus goes many places, preaching to whoever will listen. For example, near the beginning of today's passage, we find Jesus preaching. And from other parts of Mark, we know that in his preaching Jesus draws people's attention to the Scriptures, especially the teachings of the great Jewish prophets. To Jesus, the Old Testament isn't old at all. To

Jesus, the Hebrew Scriptures are a contemporary source of strength and hope. They are full of current relevance. So in his preaching, Jesus helps make those Scriptures live. Through them, he brings encouragement to all who will listen.

Another way that people in this Gospel learn from Jesus is through his parables. Like many of the best Jewish teachers, Jesus is a great storyteller. He tells stories not just for entertainment but because they are a powerful way to make a point. They are teaching tools. They are easy for people to remember and easy for people to share with others. Anyone who reads very far in the Gospel of Mark will encounter some of Jesus' dramatic parables.

A third way that people in the Gospel of Mark learn from Jesus is through his performances. That is, people learn from Jesus' deeds. Many of the Jewish prophets used dramatic actions to convey important truths. What they said and did in public was a teaching tool. In the same way, people learn from Jesus' actions. In the Gospel of Mark, Jesus deliberately takes advantage of public situations to dramatize those things that he longs for the troubled people of Palestine to understand. For example, in today's passage, we'll see Jesus turning a public situation into a powerful teaching tool.

PART THREE: As we look at the Gospel of Mark, we need to remember that this Gospel was never intended to be a complete biography of Jesus. Nor is it a fully detailed history. Rather, it's a wonderfully dramatic story, a story with the power to change lives for the better. We can be sure that it's not the full story of Jesus. Most of what Jesus preached is surely not here. Most of Jesus' parables are surely missing. And most of his teaching performances have been skipped over. There wouldn't be room for everything.

What the writer of Mark does is to carefully select those sermons and parables and public encounters that will work together in an effective way to convey what Mark feels most needs to be conveyed to the people of his day—people who live in poverty and oppression and political turmoil, probably about thirty-five years after the death of Jesus.

From Mark's perspective, every story that's included is included for a reason. Every story is included because of its great importance to what Mark wants to convey to those people who will read or hear this Gospel. Mark isn't writing in a vacuum. He knows and understands the needs and hopes and fears of the people he is addressing.

So each time we read a new passage from the Gospel of Mark, we can ask ourselves, Why did the author want to include this? What is it about this particular story or teaching or parable that will speak so strongly to the people of Mark's day?

When we think about passages from the Gospel this way, we are better able to grasp Mark's theology. We are better able sense his understanding of what the message of Jesus is all about. And this allows the passage to have a greater impact on our lives as well.

PART FOUR: In this week's passage from Mark, we'll find people talking about sins being forgiven. To understand this passage, we need to understand that in Jesus' day, sin has a very broad meaning. We can see something of this when we think about the Lord's Prayer.

In some translations of the Lord's Prayer, it says, "Forgive us our sins as we forgive those who have sinned against us." In other translations, it says, "Forgive us our debts as we forgive our debtors." And in still other translations, it says, "Forgive us our trespasses as we forgive those who trespass against us."

All of these translations are different sides of the same concept. For the Jews of Palestine, many things fall into the category of sins. Sin includes violations of God's moral commands, unpaid financial obligations, economic debts, trespassing on others' legal rights, disobeying rules laid down by the religious or political establishment, and a lot more.

Sin is a very broad category, and its broadness has terrible ramifications. In Jesus' day, people who are ill are thought to have sinned in some way, even if it isn't obvious how. Or perhaps their parents or grandparents have sinned. And thus it is thought that they can and should be excluded from religious, economic, and community life. To be a sinner is almost like being trapped forever. The effect is devastating.

PART FIVE: In this week's passage, we'll also encounter the Gospel's first use of the term "Son of Man." This term appears many times in the Gospels, almost always on the lips of Jesus. We modern Christians sometimes misunderstand what this term means. We may think that it's a special, exclusive name for Jesus. Or we may think that it somehow conveys his divinity. Both ideas are wrong.

In the language of Jesus, "son of man" means literally something like "offspring of Adam." It is a term that conveys someone's deep and full humanity, not divinity. In fact, some recent English translations of Scripture translate it as "the human one," and this probably comes closer to conveying its true meaning.

But even when translated as "the human one," it isn't a title exclusively for Jesus. We know, for example, that some of the Hebrew prophets used the term as a way of describing themselves. The prophet Ezekiel often called himself "the son of man." It was a way of identifying himself with the line of Adam, the prize of God's creation (see Ezekiel 2:1-3 for an example).

The Book of Daniel also uses the term "son of man." It appears in one of Daniel's futuristic visions (Daniel 7:13-14). In this vision, Daniel sees a "son of man," or a "human one," challenging the power and glory of the world's nations.

In the Gospels, Jesus often talks about "the Son of Man," and he often uses the term as a description of himself. Maybe that's because he wants to include himself in that group of human beings who truly understand that they, like Adam, have been created by God. And maybe he wants to include himself in that group of human beings who understand that they, like Adam, have a calling—and that calling inevitably challenges all those governments and dominions that follow their own ways rather than the ways of God.

In the New Testament, it is only Jesus who uses this term. The Jewish Christians who wrote the other books in our New Testament use many terms for Jesus. They call him "Messiah" and "Savior" and "Son of God" and other terms of praise. But never do they themselves call him "Son of Man" or "the human one."

Perhaps these early Christians understand something that we too need to understand. They understand that "the son of man" includes Jesus but is not limited to him. Jesus is the perfect offspring of Adam, but we too in our own way are the offspring of Adam. Jesus, as the Son of Man, is an example to us of what being human really means.

TEXT TO READ: MARK 2:1-2

COMMENT ON THE TEXT: At the end of Mark 1, Jesus heals a leper. He tells the leper to go straight to the priests and show them what God has done. Jesus longs to bring change to the corrupt religious establishment. But instead of obeying Jesus, the leper goes about the countryside, telling the common people of his cleansing. The common folks are thrilled, but the priests, who feel threatened by it all, are enraged. This causes great sorrow and difficulty for Jesus. Because of the commotion, he goes into seclusion in barren places in the countryside, places where the priests have less influence.

Now, however, "after some days," Jesus ventures back into the city of Capernaum, near the Sea of Galilee. The house he goes to may be the home of Peter and Andrew, where he has stayed before. It is undoubtedly a small house, more like a hut, the home of a poor fishing family.

It is soon "noised" about that Jesus has returned, and great crowds gather around the house, more than will ever fit inside. And Jesus "preached the word unto them." He shows them the great promises of the prophets, about how God won't forsake them, about how the hungry will be filled with good things, and about how the grip of the oppressor will be broken.

TEXT TO READ: MARK 2:3-4

COMMENT ON THE TEXT: People's hearts are strengthened and encouraged as they hear Jesus' preaching, and when hearts are strengthened and encouraged, things begin to happen. Soon four people bring to Jesus "one sick of the palsy." Literally this means someone who is paralyzed, someone who can't move on his or her own.

In Jesus' day, someone afflicted with paralysis is thought to be a terrible sinner. They or their parents or their grandparents, it is thought, must have committed some terrible sin. Perhaps they violated God's moral law. Maybe they borrowed money and failed to repay it. Maybe they trespassed on some obscure legal requirement set down by the governing authorities.

In Jesus' day, people don't understand the causes of disease in the same way we do. So in their struggle to understand sickness and disability, they often attribute the worst diseases to some kind of sin.

To associate with such sinners is to risk having their sin rub off on you. So they are often left alone, to beg or even to die. Disease is a terribly destructive and divisive thing. Yet here are four people from the city of Capernaum who are willing to believe something else—and they are ready to act on their belief. They don't shun their friend because of his apparent sin. Instead, they gather him up on a crude stretcher, literally, a bedroll of the kind that only the poorest people use.

In Jesus' day, bedrolls are usually infested with fleas and mites. This man's bedroll may have often been soaked in sweat and urine. As a disabled, paralyzed man, he may also be a bit disfigured. He likely stinks. But these four friends gather him up and bring him to Jesus.

When they get there, the house is full. Even the area around the door is jammed. We don't know what they want or expect by bringing this paralyzed man to Jesus. Perhaps all they want is to bring him into the sound of Jesus' voice, so that he too, in his paralysis, can hear the encouraging words of Scripture. Perhaps they hope that he too can hear of the great love of God for all people. But they can't get close enough.

So these four friends climb onto the roof of the little hut where Jesus is preaching. It may have been a little like a Navajo hogan, a small, round house made of sticks and mud. The King James Bible says that they broke up the roof, but the text literally says that they "unroofed the roof," probably by digging through the mud structure. And when they have made an opening, they lower their paralyzed friend through the roof, so that he too might feel and hear the hope that Jesus brings.

TEXT TO READ: MARK 2:5

FIRST COMMENT ON THE TEXT: When the paralyzed man is lowered through the mud roof of the little house, two remarkable things happen. The first thing that happens is that Jesus sees the "faith" of these four friends who have brought the paralyzed man to Jesus. They have broken through social and religious taboos. Not only have they understood the love of God for the broken and the despairing, but they are willing to act on that understanding.

We're told elsewhere in the Scriptures that faith without works is dead (James 2:17). And the actions of these four friends show a faith that is thriving and alive. No wonder Jesus praises them. They have been willing to help somebody, somebody who many consider unworthy.

By praising their faith, Jesus seems to be reminding us that if there is to be a "balm in Gilead" (Jeremiah 8:22), then we need to live as people of faith. And as people of faith, he seems to say, we will surely foster that balm by helping somebody. Maybe even somebody no one else will help.

SECOND COMMENT ON THE TEXT: Then the second remarkable thing happens. Jesus turns to this smelly, disfigured, paralyzed man and says,

"Son." The word that Mark quotes Jesus as using is an affectionate term, such as a father might use for a dear child. So immediately we sense a spirit of great love coming from Jesus.

And then, after addressing the paralyzed man so tenderly, Jesus makes an amazing pronouncement: "Thy sins be forgiven thee." It isn't a request. It isn't a future hope. It is a present declaration: "Son, your sins and debts and trespasses and all your financial obligations, whatever they may be—they are all forgiven, wiped out, set aside. No more do you owe anyone anything."

In a few quick words and without the slightest hesitation, Jesus declares that this man's slate is clean. It isn't an outwardly good man to whom Jesus makes this declaration. Because of his paralysis, this man seems to be nothing but a sinner. Because he hasn't been able to work, he is undoubtedly in the debt of many. Yet Jesus declares his debts and sins and trespasses forgiven.

This is a shocking and startling thing for Jesus to do. But Jesus is taking a dramatic public situation and turning it into an important teaching performance. There is something important that he is trying to teach—something so important that Mark wants to include this scene in his Gospel.

By declaring that this smelly, disfigured paralytic is forgiven, Jesus seems to be reminding us that if there is to be a balm in Gilead, then we, like Jesus, must begin to forgive—not just somebody but everybody. Even those who seem, from their external appearance, to be great debtors and great sinners.

For Discussion: In our world, whom do we find it most difficult to forgive? How can we be more forgiving?

Note: If you are breaking this session in half due to time constraints, this might be a good place to stop. When you resume, you can reestablish the context by first rereading Mark 2:1-5.

TEXT TO READ: MARK 2:6-7

COMMENT ON THE TEXT: Some scribes, who perpetuate the status quo and who owe their status more to Rome than to God, are sitting nearby. They find themselves deeply disturbed. They feel that what Jesus has declared is "blasphemy," for only God, they reason, can forgive sins.

We often make the same mistake. We fear anything that rattles those social, economic, and religious systems that we have become familiar with. People are supposed to honor their debts. People are supposed to pay for their sins. People are supposed to make amends for their trespasses. For someone to come along and flatly declare that the worst sins and debts and trespasses are forgiven would make some of us alarmed as well.

Sometimes it's more comfortable for us to hold onto those debts that people owe us. Sometimes it's more comfortable for us to hold grudges over those who have wronged us. Sometimes we'd rather insist that others pay for what they have done and leave the forgiving, if there is to be any, to God.

But the Gospel of Mark seems to be telling us that all such thinking comes from "the reasoning in [our own] hearts" rather than from the Spirit of God. For if there is to be a balm in Gilead, we can't leave the forgiving to God. What Jesus did was not blasphemy, as the scribes think in their hearts. Forgiveness is not limited to God. Forgiveness is for us all. It's for each of us to receive, for each of us to give.

TEXT TO READ: MARK 2:8-11

FIRST COMMENT ON THE TEXT: We're told that Jesus perceives "in his spirit" what the scribes are reasoning in their hearts. Jesus knows that such thoughts reflect the way of the flesh, not the way of God. Thoughts such as theirs stifle the healing balm that is so needed, both in Jesus' day and in our own. So immediately Jesus speaks, challenging their protection of the rigid walls that so often oppress "the sin-sick soul."

He asks the scribes which they think is easier—to declare a paralyzed man's sins and debts forgiven or to order him to get up and walk? The answer, of course, is that neither is easy. To the scribes, both seem like impossibilities.

But then, to show the scribes that the Son of Man does indeed have power on earth to forgive sins, he tells the paralyzed man to get up and walk. The "Son of Man" is Jesus, but it's more than Jesus. For it's all of us who are the offspring of Adam. It's all of us who are human. It's all of us who have been fashioned by God's hand, designed to live in God's way. It's all of us who are clay in the hands of the Potter.

Jesus' performance before the scribes and before the common people of Capernaum is designed to teach that forgiveness is not something that belongs to God alone. For we too as human beings have the power to forgive. And we too are called to forgive. Not just little sins. Not just the debts and trespasses of good, upstanding folk. No, we as the offspring of Adam have the power and the calling to forgive everybody, even smelly, disfigured outcasts, deep in debt and awash in sin.

This story shows us religious scribes who are "reasoning in their hearts" that only God can forgive moral sins, personal wrongs, violent crime, economic debts, and legal trespasses. Then the narrative shows us Jesus declaring that they have reasoned wrong. The lesson of the Gospel is that we, as religious people, must be careful not to reason as the scribes reason—or we too will be found wrong. We who have been created in the image of God are to practice God's grace and mercy in all of our relationships with others.

For Discussion: Why do Christians today put so much emphasis on Jesus forgiving sins "on the cross" when he was practicing and declaring forgiveness from the beginning of the Gospel? Do you think that Jesus' death at the hands of the state was the beginning of his forgiving ministry, its natural conclusion, or something else entirely?

SECOND COMMENT ON THE TEXT: It's not just the scribes that Jesus addresses in this part of the story. It's also the paralyzed man. To this disreputable, disfigured, and disabled individual, Jesus turns and says, "Arise, and take up thy bed, and go thy way into thine house."

Some Christians these days are fond of quoting the words "Let go and let God." And in some circumstances, that can be good advice. But in this story, Mark reminds us that sometimes God needs us to take action as well. To the paralyzed man, Jesus says, "Take up thy bed." To the paralyzed man, Jesus says, "Pick up that thing that has held you down, and let it hold you no more." To the paralyzed man, Jesus says, "Take your burden to the Lord and leave it there!"

Sometimes, like the man in this story, we too can be paralyzed. We too can be incapacitated. We too can be unable to take those liberating actions that are needed in our disreputable, disfigured, and disabled lives. We can find ourselves afraid to take those steps that are so needed if we are ever to break free from whatever has bound us and disabled us and forced us to live on the edge of God's world. So to us too, Jesus says, "Take up your bed. Pick up that oppressive burden that has so weighed you down. Live with it no longer."

THIRD COMMENT ON THE TEXT: An old hymn written by Charles A. Tindley is right. We have to "leave our burdens" with the Lord. But we can't leave them there until we pick them up and take them there. In this story from the Gospel of Mark, Jesus invites a distressed and disabled man to go his own way into his own home and to enjoy the freedom and rest that should be his. But before he can go, before he can experience that liberation, he has to take up his bed. He has to pick up his burden—and let it be a burden no longer.

Often, it's hard to pick up our burden. It's hard to take up our bed. Those things that weigh us down are often tied up with our deepest fears. We can become so intimidated by others that we hesitate forever to join hands with God. Even though, as an old hymn says, "love lifted me," we nervously hang on to our bed. So to all who are paralyzed, in whatever way, the Gospel of Mark says, "Take up your bed. Take up your burden. Be held down no longer."

The last step in fostering a healing balm, Jesus seems to say, is to fear nobody. We take up all that holds us down, whatever others may say. If we are to walk in our own way to our own home—if we are to arise, tall and free—if we are to experience love lifting us, then we need to summon from within the courage to take up our bed and walk.

For Discussion: What are the fears and burdens that most hold us down? What are the beds that Jesus may be asking us to take up?

TEXT TO READ: MARK 2:12

COMMENT ON THE TEXT: The paralyzed man, overloaded with sins and debts and fears, overwhelmed with burdens too great to bear, hears the words of Jesus. He feels a Holy Spirit moving deep within his soul, fortifying him and empowering him. And he hears a voice, as from God, whispering, "Be of good courage." Immediately, without hesitation, he arises. He takes up his bed, and he walks.

The people who see it glorify God, for God is the love lifter. God is the fear breaker. God is the courage giver. Jesus has performed before them the truth of who God is and who they are and what they can be. Through this dramatic demonstration of faith and love and forgiveness and the overcoming of fears, they see what they never saw before. And as we read, we sense that they may never see life in the old way again.

For Discussion: Have there been events and actions that have changed our ways of seeing? Can we remember some of those key times when God's love became so evident around us that we too were brought into a new way of seeing and understanding? What were some of those times?

TEXT TO READ: MARK 2:13-15

FIRST COMMENT ON THE TEXT: After the dramatic encounter with the paralyzed man, Jesus goes back to the Sea of Galilee. The crowds follow. On the way, Jesus comes across a man named Levi, "sitting at the receipt of custom."

This man is a toll taker and a scoundrel. He is a Jew who has sold out not only to the Romans but also to his own greed. He sits there near the sea and imposes taxes on those who pass by: farmers and fishing people, folks living on the edge of disaster. They have little money and little hope. But he insists on stealing a major portion of what they have. He's a shake-down artist who grabs from the poor, keeping a portion for himself and passing on the bulk of it to the rich elites who are exploiting the people.

People like Levi have no morals, no ethics, no scruples. They terrorize people, threatening to call in Roman soldiers if they don't pay up. If anyone in Palestine is despised, it is people like Levi. But Jesus goes up to this despicable scoundrel and says, "Follow me." The Jesus that we meet in the Gospel of Mark longs for all people to be changed. He excludes no one, for he sees the God-given possibilities in everyone. And when Levi hears Jesus' call, he takes up his burden—his job, his status, his whole way of living—and follows Jesus.

SECOND COMMENT ON THE TEXT: Jesus then goes to a meal in Levi's house, and he has Levi invite all the "publicans and sinners" he knows. This is like sitting down for a meal with a collection of drug dealers, pimps, and brutally racist police officers—people who on the surface deserve not the smallest ounce of respect. But Jesus is determined to change them, love them, and show them God's way.

We're tempted to write certain people out of God's arms. We're tempted to say that there are people in this world whom no one ought to embrace. But through his performance, through his actions, Jesus is telling us that if you want a healing balm running deep and strong in Gilead, then you need to love anybody. No matter who they are. No matter what they do. No matter how strong the hate you feel for them.

For Discussion: When the poor of Capernaum see Jesus approaching Levi, the shakedown artist, what emotions do you think might go through their hearts? What might Peter and Andrew and James and John think as they join Jesus at the dinner table with a whole houseful of the very people who have made their lives in the fishing business so terrifying?

THIRD COMMENT ON THE TEXT: In these first fifteen verses of Mark 2, we see Jesus performing for us. Through his words and actions in these dramatic encounters, we learn that if we are to foster a healing balm in Gilead, if we are to be true children of Adam and true clay in the hands of the Potter, then we need to:

> love ANYBODY, like the Jesus who eats with a houseful of shake-down artists;
>
> fear NOBODY, like the paralyzed man, who has the courage to take up his bed and walk;
>
> help SOMEBODY, like the four people who bring the smelly, disfig-ured man to Jesus;
>
> forgive EVERYBODY, like Jesus instructed the scribes.

In these fifteen verses, we've seen Jesus identifying himself with us by calling himself the Son of Man, the human one, the offspring of Adam. And we've encountered the heart of Jesus' message for all of us human ones—a message of faith and love and forgiveness, a message with healing and transforming power, a message he urgently wants everyone to hear.

For Discussion: What do you think it was about these stories that Mark found so important for the lives, struggles, and fears of his first readers? What do you think he hoped these stories would do for them? What should these accounts say to us?

SESSION 2

AND HE SAID UNTO
THEM, WHY ARE YE
SO FEARFUL? HOW IS
IT THAT YE HAVE
NO FAITH?
—MARK 4:40

LIKE A SHIP UPON THE SEA

MARK 4:33-41

SETTING THE STAGE

Early in Mark 4, Jesus goes to the Sea of Galilee. There he gets into a boat, and from the boat he teaches a large crowd of people. His teaching on this day is all in parables, for we're told that "without a parable spake he not unto them." And presumably, from what Mark tells us, there are many more parables told than are included here.

We're told that after teaching the crowd in parables, Jesus meets privately with the twelve disciples and with other sisters and brothers. These are his most committed followers, the ones he has called his true family. And to this smaller and more intimate group, he has "expounded all things." He has explained the parables. He has spoken freely. He has

14

passionately conveyed to them the heart of his message. He has sown the seed in their hearing in the hope that its roots will go deep and bear abundant fruit. How well that seed has or has not transformed their hearts will soon be evident.

TEXT TO READ: MARK 4:33-35

FIRST COMMENT ON THE TEXT: In the scene that Mark unfolds for us, after a long day of teaching, when evening has come, Jesus turns to his closest followers and says, "Let us pass over unto the other side."

The Sea of Galilee is a freshwater lake. At its largest point, it's about seven miles wide and maybe twelve miles long. The city of Capernaum, which has been the center of Jesus' ministry, is on the northwest side of the lake. The other side of the lake, the eastern side, is more Gentile in character. Many people living there are not Jewish in their faith—and not Jewish in their practice.

And yet, like those who have already followed Jesus, the people on the other side of the lake are poor. They're peasants. They fear the Roman army. And they fear local political thugs who terrorize their daily lives. The people on the other side of the lake are Palestinian, not Jewish. So they are often viewed with suspicion, even by the poor peasants of Galilee, with whom they have so much in common.

SECOND COMMENT ON THE TEXT: As evening falls, Jesus tells his closest followers that he wants to pass over to the other side—to that distant shore where so many foreigners live, to that distant shore where so many people live in misery, to that distant shore where God's love is so little known, to that distant shore where the seed has not yet been planted.

It's a long way across the waters. Night has fallen. Storms can be fierce. And the people on the other side are strangers. They're different. They aren't even a part of the same religious tradition. In fact, they're seen by many as being outside God's circle of concern.

Yet as the shadows of evening grow long, after a full day of planting the seed, Jesus turns to his closest followers and says, "Let us—not just me but all of us—let us go over to the other side, to a distant shore, to a strange place. And let's not wait until later. Let's go right now."

For Discussion: If you had been in the group with Jesus that evening, what emotions would have gone through your heart? What kinds of things today does God ask us to do that feel as difficult as crossing in the night to the other side, over a wide and dangerous sea?

TEXT TO READ: MARK 4:36

COMMENT ON THE TEXT: Mark shows us the disciples sending the multitude away. Then he tells us that the disciples take Jesus, "even as he was," into a boat. After a long day of teaching, Jesus may be tired. His body may be hot and sweaty. But he has no desire to go home. He has no desire to take care of personal business. He is ready to cross to the other side. So the disciples nervously take him with them into a boat.

But it's not just one boat that sets out. One boat isn't enough, for by this time Jesus has a growing group of disciples and followers. We're told that a whole collection of boats sets out together—a company of little ships, setting out through the night, with little in the way of lights except maybe the moon and stars.

We can imagine what must be going through their hearts. Not only has Jesus asked them to do a difficult thing at an awkward time, but also, when they make it to the other side, it's a place that they aren't sure they want to be.

For Discussion: Do you think the fact that there were enough people to fill multiple boats makes the journey easier or harder for Jesus' followers? Why? What lessons can we draw from this for our lives as Christians?

TEXT TO READ: MARK 4:37

COMMENT ON THE TEXT: If the moon and stars were out when Jesus' followers set out, they quickly disappear. A great wind blows across the water. A storm is rising. Gales are howling. Waves are lashing the boat to and fro.

The disciples and all those who have followed Jesus are frantically trying to bail water out of their wooden vessels. But they can't keep up with the wind and the waves. Water pours in faster than they can cast it out, and Mark tells us that before long, the battered boats are rapidly filling with water.

And it's not just one boat that's in danger but a whole company of boats, carrying all of Jesus' disciples and all of his closest followers. The wind and the waves that batter the boats on this journey to the other side are threatening the entire family of believers. Every seed that has heard the word is on the sea together. And in the picture that Mark paints, it looks for all the world like they'll go down together.

For Discussion: Today, when we as the people of God cross to the other side with Jesus—when we set out with him to do the difficult thing, the unpopular thing, the courageous thing—what kind of storms beat against our ships? What kinds of storms threaten to take us down together?

TEXT TO READ: MARK 4:38

COMMENT ON THE TEXT: We don't know what kinds of boats are used in those days on the Sea of Galilee, except that they are made of wood and designed, most likely, for fishing. But seemingly there is a spot near the back of the boat where Jesus has curled up and gone to sleep. Some people imagine that it's a sheltered spot, under a cover of some kind. But there's no evidence for that.

And if the boat is filling with water, if the wind is howling, if the boat is rocking to and fro, if rain is falling, if thunder is clapping, if waves are crashing over the sides, and if the whole wooden vessel feels like it's about to break apart, then it's not likely that the spot that Jesus has chosen is in any way quiet. He's as much in the midst of the storm as those disciples and followers who have accompanied him. Yet he sleeps. The storm rages. But it doesn't faze him.

Frantic, some of the disciples finally shake Jesus awake. They can't believe that he's been sleeping. They can't believe that he's not scared out of his wits. They can't believe that he can ignore the storm that's beating down so hard.

"Master!" or "Teacher!" they cry, shouting over the howling wind and waves. "Don't you care that we're all about to die? Don't you care that this boat is going down—and us with it?" They can't believe what he's been doing while the storm is raging. It's too amazing.

For Discussion: What do you think the disciples are thinking as they wake Jesus? Is their question a statement of desperation, or might there be a sense of accusation in it as well? What kinds of situations make us go to God with some of these same thoughts and feelings?

COMMENT ON JESUS' ACTIONS, PART ONE: One of the most puzzling things about this dramatic story is the question of why Jesus would sleep through the storm and leave his disciples and followers to battle it alone.

When they rouse him, the disciples ask, "Carest thou not that we perish?" But the way they ask the question implies that they already know the answer. Of course, Jesus cares. His whole life with them has been a demonstration of compassion.

So is Jesus simply exhausted? Is he so tired from his day of teaching that he just needs to sleep? Maybe, but it's not likely that he is any more tired than the disciples, who have been up all day as well and are now having to row a boat through a storm. And even if a person were exhausted, how could you sleep through a storm like this? It seems more likely that Jesus, through his actions in the boat, is deliberately dramatizing a truth for his disciples.

COMMENT ON JESUS' ACTIONS, PART TWO: Throughout Mark, we see Jesus teaching his followers in a variety of ways. He teaches through his preaching and through his parables. But he also teaches through his performances.

Like other Jewish prophets, the Jesus that we encounter in Mark's Gospel has a flair for dramatic action. Not just for drama's sake, but to teach and illustrate a point in a dramatic and effective way.

So it seems likely that by sleeping through a raging storm, Jesus is teaching his disciples something. This is a performance that they will not soon forget.

Earlier in Mark's Gospel, Jesus encounters a paralyzed man, "sick of the palsy" (Mark 2:1-12). The man can't walk, and he is lowered into the room where Jesus is by four of his friends. Jesus commends the friends for their great faith, and then, declaring the man's sins forgiven, he tells the man to take up his bed and walk.

The bed in that story is symbolic of what holds the man down. Sin and sickness are all mixed up in his mind, and he has been letting the bed fill his soul with terror and dread. So Jesus tells the man that his sins are forgiven. And as a forgiven child of God, he need not be bound by that which has been holding him back and holding him down. "Take up your bed," says Jesus, "pick up that thing which has filled you with fear, pick up that thing that has disabled you and diminished you—and walk."

By carrying the bed with him, the man becomes the master of that which has enslaved him. By carrying the bed with him, the man breaks free of fear and walks in faith.

COMMENT ON JESUS' ACTIONS, PART THREE: Perhaps in this story of a raging storm, Jesus is demonstrating that same spirit of faith. Perhaps Jesus is showing his disciples that "when the storms of life are raging," you must have the faith to believe that God is standing right by your side.

By deliberately sleeping through the storm, Jesus shows what it means to take up your bed and walk—but in this case, the burden of fear that he lifts is not a bed but a storm. Through his performance this night, Jesus teaches his disciples to take up the storms and sail.

The point he wants them to learn is that fear has no place in the life of faith. A seed has been planted. It may be slow in coming to harvest. There may be storms and crises along the way. We will lie down and rise up, night after night, day after day, not knowing how the seed is managing to grow.

But if we wait with faith, if we wait believing that God is standing right by our side, the tiny seed that God has planted will grow into a mighty tree, taller than any other tree on the face of this earth. And that mighty tree will stand as a refuge and a stronghold for all who are in need.

Take up your terrors, Jesus seems to be saying, take them up—and then run on in the pathway of faith. Don't let fear hold you back, for "the kingdom of God is at hand" (Mark 1:15).

For Discussion: Earlier in Mark 4, Jesus tells a parable about the word of God being planted in four different kinds of soil, with four different kinds of responses. There was the hard soil that the seed couldn't penetrate. There was the shallow, rocky soil, where the seed flourished at first but then faded as soon as hardship came. There was the soil choked with thorns and riches and lusts of this world. And there was the good soil where the roots went deep and the seed bore abundant fruit. By their actions in the storm, what kind of soil do the disciples seem to have?

COMMENT ON BIBLICAL CONNECTIONS: The Gospel of Mark shows us a Jesus who is deeply rooted in the Hebrew Scriptures. And this story is no exception.

One of the great portraits of God's steadfast love is found in Psalm 107. That psalm talks about the hungry being fed. It talks about prisoners being set free. It talks about the sick being healed. And then it talks about people who "went down to the sea in ships." A "stormy wind" comes up, with great waves rocking their boat up and down. "Their courage melted away in their calamity," says the psalm. "They reeled and staggered like drunkards, and were at their wits' end. Then they cried to the LORD in their trouble, and the LORD brought them out from their distress; he made the storm be still, and the waves of the sea were hushed" (Psalm 107:23-29, NRSV).

This story in Mark is a dramatic enactment of the very scene that Psalm 107 describes. It's Mark's way of reminding his readers that when we follow Jesus to the other side of the sea, when we walk with Jesus into strange and unknown territory, when we do the hard things that God sometimes calls us to, great storms may arise.

But even when those storms are raging, we should take up our fears and walk. Like Jesus, we can sleep, as it were, through even the most dramatic storm, for we know that there is a Lord who hears our cry and who will stand by us every day, whether the sea is calm or the waves are crashing, whether the wind is still or the gales are raging.

TEXT TO READ: MARK 4:39-40

FIRST COMMENT ON THE TEXT: Seeing the frantic look on his disciples' faces, Jesus commands the winds and the waves to be quiet. Suddenly there is a great calm.

Through his words and the response of the wind and the waves, Jesus shows his disciples not a new truth but an old truth. He shows them that the storm is strong. But God is stronger. From the minute that the winds began blowing and from the moment that the waves began rising, there was a God who was watching. There was a God whose word could still the storm. And there was a God whose word is greater far than any wind that blows our way.

In Mark's Gospel, the story of the storm comes just after we're told that Jesus has "expounded all things to his disciples" (Mark 4:34). By now, he hopes they've understood. By now, he hopes the seed is working its way deep into their hearts. But the soil is still shallow and rocky. And when the winds blow, they flounder. "Why are ye so fearful?" he asks. "How is it that ye have so little faith?"

SECOND COMMENT ON THE TEXT: In *The Strength to Love*, Dr. Martin Luther King Jr. told about speaking at a Monday evening meeting somewhere in the South after a tense week of civil rights struggles. He felt depressed and fearful. At the end of the meeting, a woman in the church called him to her. She hugged him and asked what was the matter. He tried to deny there was any problem, but she wouldn't be fooled. His speaking hadn't been as strong as usual that night. She wondered if the white folks were getting to him or if the black folks weren't standing behind him strong enough. She reminded him that she and the others in the meeting were behind him all the way—and even if they fell by the wayside, God was going to take care of him.

From that night on, wrote Dr. King, whenever he was discouraged, whenever fear welled up inside him, whenever the storms seemed to be too much, he remembered those simple words that have been repeated over and over by so many, "God's gonna take of you."

The spirit that Jesus calls us to is the spirit that is reflected in an old motto that people used to put up on the walls of their homes:

> *Fear knocked at the door.*
> *Faith answered.*
> *There was no one there.*

TEXT TO READ: MARK 4:41

COMMENT ON THE TEXT: Jesus stills the storm and shows the disciples that they had no need for fear. Yet, through Jesus' actions, the disciples soon find themselves awash in a new fear: a fear that this Jesus is more than they imagined. "What manner of man is this," they ask, "that even wind and waves obey him?"

It's a question they will continue to struggle with, for they haven't yet understood this is more than a man from Nazareth. God's hand has come close. It has come as close to their lives and their hearts as it has come to ours. The ways of God are taking root in their midst, just as the ways of God are taking root in ours.

We can remain shackled to our beds. We can remain terrorized by our fears. We can remain paralyzed by every evil that the powers of Satan throw our way. Or . . . we can take hold of that One who is stronger than the strongest and greater than the greatest. And we can walk in faith with that One whose power and love go beyond even our deepest longings.

Charles A. Tindley expressed the same thought in "Stand by Me," one of his most famous hymns:

> *When the world is tossing me, like a ship upon the sea,*
> *Thou who rulest wind and water, stand by me!*

SESSION 3

AND WHEN THE SABBATH DAY
WAS COME, HE BEGAN TO TEACH
IN THE SYNAGOGUE: AND MANY
HEARING HIM WERE ASTONISHED,
SAYING, FROM WHENCE HATH
THIS MAN THESE THINGS? . . . IS
NOT THIS THE CARPENTER, THE
SON OF MARY. . . ? AND THEY
WERE OFFENDED AT HIM.
—MARK 6:2-3

WHAT FOLKS SAY ABOUT ME

MARK 6:1-6

SETTING THE STAGE

Jesus and his disciples are walking tall. They've seen the power of faith in one dramatic situation after another. They've met the most unlikely people reaching out to God with faith and not fear. Storms have been stilled. A violent maniac has been transformed not by chains but by love. A woman with an endless hemorrhage has reached out in faith and been made whole. A synagogue leader has broken with his social group and come to Jesus in faith. And his daughter, lying on the doorway of death, has been brought back to health and strength.

But Jesus and his disciples are about to be brought low. They will feel the pain of rejection and scorn. Their hearts will be mocked. Their wisdom will be questioned. Their character will be belittled. And this cynical criticism will come from the very ones who should have been claiming Jesus as their own.

BACKGROUND TEXT TO READ: MARK 3:31-35

COMMENT ON THE TEXT: Jesus seems to have had a rough time with his family. Those who are close to him are the most vocal in rejecting him. Mark first introduces Jesus' family in Mark 3. We meet a family frightened and embarrassed at what Jesus is doing. They come to get him, to take him away from his ministry, to haul him back to Nazareth. They want him out of sight.

Jesus' response is to declare that his true family is not the family he was born into but all those who "do the will of God." That's what makes a person his mother, his brother, his sister. And the clear implication is that his family—his mother, his brothers, his sisters—do not do the will of God. So Jesus at this point doesn't feel much closeness to them.

TEXT TO READ: MARK 6:1

COMMENT ON THE TEXT: After a series of amazing encounters with the power of faith, Jesus and his disciples return to Jesus' home country. Mark 1:24 has identified Jesus as a resident of Nazareth, a rural community in Galilee, incredibly small. Perhaps Jesus hopes that folk there will now have heard more about his ministry. Perhaps Jesus hopes that folk there will have heard more about the power of faith. Perhaps Jesus hopes that folk there will be more open now than they were before to his preaching about the good news of God's kingdom, which grows in their midst.

TEXT TO READ: MARK 6:2A

COMMENT ON THE TEXT: Throughout the early chapters of Mark, we find Jesus going to the local synagogues, where he teaches and preaches and shares the Jewish Scriptures that he knows so well. And when he returns to his home territory, in the area of Nazareth, he does the same. Sabbath comes, and he heads to the synagogue, as all faithful Jews would do.

For Mark, however, this synagogue visit is a major turning point. Never again, anywhere in the Gospel of Mark, will we see Jesus going to a synagogue.

This is the last time Mark will mention Jesus going to a synagogue.

For Discussion: This synagogue visit is a distressing one for Jesus, for the people who speak with him do not reflect the will of God. Their spirit is the opposite of what God wants. They fail to show the attitude that God calls us to. And Jesus never returns. There are people in our world who have been burned by their encounters with critical, mean-spirited Christians who have failed to speak and act in God's way. And some of these people are no longer willing to walk inside a church. They've been hurt too badly. Can you think of situations where that might have happened? What kinds of people today might have experienced that kind of rejection? What can we who want to share the true spirit of Christ do to reach out in love to those who have been mistreated by God's people?

TEXT TO READ: MARK 6:2B-3

FIRST COMMENT ON THE TEXT: Those from his home country who hear Jesus teaching and preaching and sharing the Scriptures are "astonished" and "offended" at what they hear. He speaks the truth, but it's a truth they don't want to hear.

The text of these verses includes four questions that they ask. These are not serious questions. These are mocking questions. These are questions used to belittle Jesus. These questions are raised as a way of dismissing what he has to say and the "mighty works" he has done.

The spirit of contempt that lies behind these verses doesn't come through as strongly in most English translations as it might if we could read these verses in Greek, the language in which they are originally written. For example, in each of the first three questions, there is a reference to "this man" or "him" or "this" person, and in all three of these questions, the Greek word that is used is one that often carries a feeling of contempt. Its meaning is more like "this guy" rather than "this man."

The tone of the first question is something like, "Where did this guy get these ideas?" There is a very casual, even disrespectful spirit to each of the questions that is raised.

SECOND COMMENT ON THE TEXT: In addition, when the people ask if this guy isn't just a carpenter, the "son of Mary," there is an implication, in how it is worded, that they consider him a bastard. By asking if he isn't the son of his mother, rather than the son of his father, it is almost like the people are calling Jesus a mocking name.

In Jesus' day, people don't have last names in the way that we do today. And it is normal to refer to someone as the child of his or her father, even if the father is dead. When you describe someone as the child of his or her mother, it is like saying, "You don't have a father." It's a put-down. It's demeaning. It's not kind or polite.

In some of today's gospel songs, there are references to being "buked" and "scorned" and "talked about," and many people today have experienced this kind of rejection. But the Gospel of Mark makes it clear that this is something that Jesus knew as well. He knew it firsthand, from his own people, from those who should have been his strongest supporters. And it's clear, from the Gospel, that this hurt.

For Discussion: Why do you think the residents of Nazareth are so cruel in their questions and in their put-downs? What motivates such behavior today? What's the responsibility of God's people toward those who are experiencing such rejection?

QUESTIONS ABOUT JESUS, PART ONE: Mark mentions four questions that are raised. The first two and the last two are closely related to each other. In effect there are two groups of questions here, and the Gospel of Mark has already given us the answer to each.

The first group of questions asks, "Where did this guy get all this stuff that he's saying? Where did this guy get his so-called wisdom? Where did he get the power to do these mighty works?"

In fact, Mark provides an answer to this first set of questions earlier in his Gospel.

BACKGROUND TEXT TO READ: MARK 1:9-10

QUESTIONS ABOUT JESUS, PART TWO: Mark makes the answer to the first set of questions clear. The wisdom with which Jesus speaks has come from above. And the power with which he works is the power of God's Spirit.

The second set of questions has more to do with identity. "Who is this guy? Isn't he just an ordinary construction worker? Isn't he the disreputable, bastard son of Mary? Don't his brother and sisters live with us right here in Nazareth? Who does he think he is, anyhow?"

As it turns out, Mark has already provided answers to this second set of questions as well.

BACKGROUND TEXT TO READ: MARK 1:6-7

QUESTIONS ABOUT JESUS, PART THREE: Is Jesus just the son of Mary, with all that this slur implies?

It's true that he is the offspring of Mary, and it may also be true that Mary had no husband when he was conceived. But from a theological perspective, Mark has already revealed whose child he believes Jesus is. And for Mark, that is important as well.

BACKGROUND TEXT TO READ: MARK 1:11

QUESTIONS ABOUT JESUS, PART FOUR: And what about Jesus' siblings? Aren't they just those ordinary folk living here in Nazareth?

For this question as well, Mark has provided an answer. It comes in the words of Jesus, found early in the Gospel.

BACKGROUND TEXT TO READ: MARK 3:35

For Discussion: If you had been there at the synagogue on that Sabbath, and if it had been you whom they were raising questions about, if it had been you whom they were belittling and demeaning, how would you have been feeling? What do you think is going through the hearts and minds of the disciples as all this is happening? Do you think an experience like this would shake their commitment to Jesus or cause it to be deepened? Why or why not?

TEXT TO READ: MARK 6:4

COMMENT ON THE TEXT: In Mark's drama, Jesus doesn't try to answer his critics. He doesn't defend himself. And he doesn't lash out. Surely he feels the pain of their rejection. Surely he feels the hurt of their slurs. Surely he feels the sorrow of their distance from him.

But all that we hear from Jesus is a simple explanation of a larger pattern that he believes his rejection falls into. "A prophet is seldom honored," he says, "in his own country." This may have been a common saying in Jesus' day. But in Mark's Gospel, Jesus adds to the saying, making reference as well to "his own kin" and "his own house."

Each of these additions seems to reflect the depth of Jesus' pain. Not only is he being rejected in his own country, but also he is being rejected by his own kin, meaning his extended family, and by his own house, meaning his immediate family.

Some Christians have romanticized Jesus' relationship with his family, especially his relationship with his mother. Artists through the centuries have painted pictures of an infant lovingly cradled in his mother's arms. Others have focused on images of Jesus speaking from the cross, lovingly asking John to care for his mother after he's gone.

But the picture that Mark paints of Jesus and his mother is a picture of pain and misunderstanding. It's a picture of rejection and antagonism. So the romantic images we sometimes think of don't tell the full story. Life is full of ups and downs. People draw close, and people fall away. Relationships thrive, and relationships falter. Jesus knew all of this. He knew it firsthand.

For Discussion: In Mark 4, Jesus described four kinds of earth that the seed of God's word falls on. What kind of earth does Jesus' home community seem to be? What other prophets can you think of, in more recent times, who experienced a similar rejection from those who should have known them best? What is that makes us so unaware of the good that is close at hand?

TEXT TO READ: MARK 6:5

COMMENT ON THE TEXT: The Jesus that we find in the Gospel of Mark is not all-powerful. He's not a magician. He can't wave his wand and do anything he wants whenever he wants.

The Jesus that we find in the Gospel of Mark is more like a channel, a channel through which God's power flows. And because God's power flows through him, he's stronger than the strongest evil and he's mightier than the mightiest opponent. But he's not a magician. So when faith isn't present, there's not much healing in his touch. When faith isn't present, new doors don't open. When faith isn't present, the seed doesn't grow. When faith isn't present, his mighty works are few.

According to Mark, the woman who touches Jesus' garment is made whole not by anything Jesus does but by the faith in her heart. Faith makes the way. So the fact that Jesus isn't able to do much in his home territory is a sign. It tells us that there are few people around Nazareth who have any faith. There are few people there who offer the kind of good earth in which the mighty seed of God's kingdom can be planted.

For Discussion: Why do you think there is so little faith in the territory around Nazareth? Mark sometimes portrays faith as the opposite of fear. In what way might fear have played a role in suppressing faith for the people of Nazareth?

TEXT TO READ: MARK 6:6

FIRST COMMENT ON THE TEXT: Earlier in Mark, Jesus has been amazed at the faith he has seen. There is the woman who reaches out to touch him. There are the four friends who lower a paralyzed man through the roof of a home so Jesus can heal him. There is the man with the withered hand. And there are so many other people in whom the seed has taken root.

But here, in his home territory, Jesus marvels at the lack of faith. Here he marvels that so few people are willing to reach out and take hold of what God is doing in their midst. God's kingdom is close. God's hand is near. God's power is ready to love them, embrace them, and make them whole. But they go about their daily lives, lost in their routines, lost in their despair, lost in their fear of any change in the status quo.

That lack of faith has caused them to belittle God's messenger of hope. That lack of faith has caused them to slur God's beloved one. That lack of faith has caused them to show contempt and scorn toward the gift that God has given.

Others, when they hear about Jesus, are filled with hope. They run to him, embrace him, and fall at his feet. But when the people of Nazareth hear about Jesus—what he's saying and what he's doing—they recoil in fear. Their words are filled with criticism and contempt. He's talked about in the meanest way. He's put down, rebuked, and ridiculed.

So Jesus leaves them. He moves on. He isn't bogged down by their attacks. He doesn't lose his confidence in God's mercy and love. He goes out to other villages in Galilee, villages where there will be a more receptive spirit, and there he teaches and preaches and shares the good news.

For Discussion: How can we help others and ourselves have the confidence that Jesus had, so that we aren't destroyed by criticism? How can we help others and ourselves develop the inner resources to hold to God's unchanging hand, even when we're surrounded by unbelief, even when we're faced with ridicule and contempt from those who are closest to us?

SECOND COMMENT ON THE TEXT: Jesus often tells those who are weighed down with troubles to pick up their mat and walk. He tells those around him to take up that which holds them down—and to move forward in faith.

Now, here at Nazareth, Jesus has to do the same. We see him breaking free. He could have been weighed down with grief. He could have been held back by the contempt that is shown him. He could have been burdened down by the slurs that are uttered. But instead he picks them up. He takes up that which has been piled on him—and moves forward. He walks on in faith, in the beautiful way that God has made for him.

As it turns out, Jesus' actions here are good practice for what lies ahead. For the time is coming when he will be not just slurred or questioned or treated with contempt. He will be mocked and spat upon. He will be stripped of his clothes and hung up for all to see. He will be tortured and killed. But it won't do any good. For he'll take up that cross—and move on. Even a grave won't be able to hold him.

THIRD COMMENT ON THE TEXT: The spirit that Jesus shows in this passage also comes through in a song that was recorded by Alex Bradford in 1958. Although he was a talented writer and performer, Alex Bradford was often criticized. Some people ridiculed him because he was African American. Some people scoffed at him because they thought gospel music wasn't worthy of respect. Some people laughed at him because of the distinctive way he sang. Some people ridiculed him because of the joyful way he dressed. Some people whispered that he was gay.

At times Bradford felt that everywhere he turned, people were harping at him. But as he took hold of Jesus' hand, he was able to overcome his burdens. He was able to take up the weights that had been put upon him and move forward in faith.

It was in that spirit that he wrote and recorded an autobiographical song in which he confessed that he used to worry both day and night about what folks were saying about him. But he indicates that that was before he met Christ—and before Christ set him free.

Breaking free is never easy, especially when critics do their worst. But Jesus calls us to take up our bed and walk. Jesus calls us to throw aside the social roadblocks—and move forward in God's holy way.

AND WHEN THE DAY WAS NOW FAR SPENT, HIS DISCIPLES CAME UNTO HIM, AND SAID, THIS IS A DESERT PLACE, AND NOW THE TIME IS FAR PASSED: SEND THEM AWAY, THAT THEY MAY GO INTO THE COUNTRY ROUND ABOUT . . . AND BUY THEMSELVES BREAD. —MARK 6:35-36

LISTEN TO THE LAMBS, ALL A-CRYING

MARK 6:32-44

SETTING THE STAGE

Mark is a master storyteller. He carefully fashions his Gospel so that we will see and feel who Jesus was and what his message means for us.

In Mark 6, Mark introduces a flashback. He recalls the death of John the Baptist. It's a gruesome scene. Herod decides to give himself a lavish birthday banquet. Herod is ruler of Galilee for the Romans. He has a big head and likes to think of himself as King Herod, even though his power is rather limited. He invites the powerful and the wealthy to his birthday banquet—government officials, soldiers, big landowners. Before it's over,

John the Baptist's bloody skull is brought to the banquet hall on a platter.

Mark weaves some remarkable contrasts into his Gospel. We'll see some of these same contrasts in today's text, especially if we keep in mind the story of Herod's birthday banquet.

Mark will move us. We'll start with the rich and powerful enjoying an evening of feasting and dancing and drunken orgies inside a great stone palace. From there we'll move to a country hillside, where a crowd of poor farmers and laborers gathers under an open sky. Here are the victims of those people who have been feasting at Herod's birthday bash. They're abused and ignored and exploited. And when mealtime comes, they will have nothing to eat.

Mark does not want us to miss this dramatic contrast. He moves from a great indoor banquet for the rich and powerful to a lonely hillside where the poor gather with little or nothing to eat. The first scene is a scene of vain promises, self-serving egos, and the violence of death. The second scene is a scene of faith, charity, and sharing. It's a scene of life and hope. It's a reminder of how we too should live.

TEXT TO READ: MARK 6:32

COMMENT ON THE TEXT: Jesus and his disciples are tired. They feel a need to rest for a while. They feel a need to be renewed and restored. So they go off by boat to "a desert place." Some translations say "a wilderness place." It was in the wilderness that the people of Israel, fleeing from slavery in Egypt, met God. So Jesus often goes to the wilderness when he wants to be renewed and restored by God.

For Discussion: Where do you go to be restored by God? Is there something about lonely, natural places that make it easier for us to meet God? Why or why not?

TEXT TO READ: MARK 6:33

COMMENT ON THE TEXT: Jesus has become widely known in Galilee. The common people—those who were never invited to Herod's birthday banquet—are captivated by this prophet and his gracious message that God and God's ways are close at hand. So when they see Jesus and his disciples getting into a boat, they quickly figure out where he is going.

Word spreads throughout the towns and villages. People come running from all over to gather on the shore where they figure Jesus and his disciples are heading.

Whether the boat is driven by sails or oars, we don't know. But apparently it is a quiet and leisurely trip. Jesus and his disciples enjoy a little peace and rest. But because of the slowness of their journey, when their boat arrives back on shore, a crowd has already gathered.

TEXT TO READ: MARK 6:34

FIRST COMMENT ON THE TEXT: Jesus gets out of the boat to find a great crowd gathered. He can see that these are a poor and oppressed people. There is much famine in the land. Crops fail. And what little the people have is often confiscated by rich landowners or by Herod's toll collectors who stand outside the markets and demand a share of everything for themselves.

Life is anything but easy. And the bonds that should be holding the community together are being broken. There isn't a spirit of togetherness and sharing. There isn't a spirit of common struggle. People are being broken apart, fending for themselves rather than for the common good. So Jesus looks at the people and is "moved with compassion." Literally the Greek text says that his guts are torn open. He feels their pain. He feels their struggle and the agonies they endure.

Mark says the people who come to hear Jesus are like "sheep not having a shepherd." That's a biting comment after the story of Herod's birthday banquet. Those who should be tending the flock are instead ripping it apart. The political establishment is no longer on the side of the sheep. It's on the side of the wolves. It gives itself lavish banquets while common people struggle to make it. An old spiritual has the line, "Listen to the lambs, all a-crying," and that's exactly what Jesus is doing.

The text doesn't tell us what Jesus teaches the people that afternoon. But if the rest of Mark is any clue, it's a message of compassion and hope. It's a message of God's love and grace. It's a message designed to plant the seed of faith. It's a message that God and God's ways are close at hand, if only we will reach out and take hold of that which God is doing in our midst.

SECOND COMMENT ON THE TEXT: Mark's portrait of Jesus often makes use of the great Jewish prophets. Mark shows us Jesus' deep connection to their words and to their witness. This story is no exception.

Centuries before the time of Jesus, the prophet Ezekiel condemns the leaders of his nation because they haven't tended to the needs of the common people. And the words of Ezekiel have an amazing relevance to this part of Mark's Gospel. They even use Jesus' favored name for himself, "Son of Man," which was also a favorite name of the prophet Ezekiel.

BACKGROUND TEXT TO READ: EZEKIEL 34:1-4

THIRD COMMENT ON THE TEXT: When we think about Ezekiel and about that scene at Herod's birthday banquet, and when we hear about the poor gathered in the wilderness with Jesus, it's not surprising that Mark describes the crowd as "sheep not having a shepherd."

In similar fashion, long before the time of Jesus, the Jewish prophet Hosea described Israel as a wandering spouse, one who leaves God to pursue other lovers. But then, in beautiful poetry, Hosea shares God's desire to bring the people of Israel back into a renewed relationship with the Almighty. In expressing that desire, Hosea quotes God as saying, "I will now allure her, and bring her into the wilderness, and speak tenderly to her. . . . There she shall respond as in the days of her youth, as at the time when she came out of the land of Egypt" (Hosea 2:14-15, NRSV).

In today's passage, we see that same spirit. In the wilderness, a crowd gathers. When Jesus sees them, immediately he has compassion on them. He speaks tenderly to them, as he knows God would have him do, for they are "sheep not having a shepherd."

FOURTH COMMENT ON THE TEXT: The story in Mark also brings to mind images from the Book of Isaiah, where we find these words: "Comfort, O comfort my people, says your God. Speak tenderly to Jerusalem, and cry to her that she has served her term, that her penalty is paid. . . . A voice cries out: 'In the wilderness prepare the way of the LORD, make straight in the desert a highway for our God' " (Isaiah 40:1-3, NRSV).

During Herod's banquet, the rich and the powerful outdo each other with drunken boasts. During Herod's banquet, the strong and the mighty demand that the head of God's prophet be brought on a platter.

But out in the wilderness, where a crowd has gathered around Jesus, the scene is different. In the wilderness, Jesus speaks tenderly to God's people. In the wilderness, Jesus comforts those who have been beaten down. In the wilderness, Jesus prepares the way of the Lord. In the wilderness, Jesus straightens the way for our God.

TEXT TO READ: MARK 6:35-36

COMMENT ON THE TEXT: In these days, most Jews eat their main meal in the mid to late afternoon. It is now that time of day or later. No one has eaten. Stomachs are growling. Folk have come long distances. They need food.

Unfortunately Jesus' disciples are still rather dense. They don't understand the significance of what is happening. They don't understand that Jesus is not just filled with compassion on an intellectual or emotional level. He's determined to make a real way out of no way. He's determined to act in faith, believing that God's ways are close at hand. He's determined to challenge the fend-for-yourself mentality. He's determined to show his disciples that when sheep need a shepherd, it's time to be a shepherd.

In their ignorance, the disciples come to Jesus and say, "It's getting late. The time for eating is past. We're out in the wilderness. Let's send these folk away, so that they can go off and buy themselves some bread." The disciples haven't yet understood that sheep without a shepherd need a shepherd. They haven't yet understood that God is calling us to remember the common good. The Holy One wants us to share with one another. The Holy One wants us to see that our destinies are intertwined. The Holy One wants us to know that when we tell others to fend for themselves, we inevitably are letting the weak and the lame and those who are oppressed fall between the cracks.

For Discussion: If you had been in the crowd that day and the disciples sent you away to find your own meal, what kind of message would that have conveyed to you? In what sorts of ways do we fall into the mentality of the disciples, asking people to fend for themselves rather than sharing with others for the common good? Our whole economic system seems to be built on a fend-for-yourself mentality. What do you think Jesus would say about the economic spirit that rules our world?

TEXT TO READ: MARK 6:37

COMMENT ON THE TEXT: When the disciples suggest sending the people away to get their own food, Jesus immediately turns to them and gives them a simple command: "Give them something to eat."

The disciples are confused. At first they think Jesus is telling them to go buy bread in a neighboring town. In shock, they protest. It will take two hundred denarii to buy enough bread for a crowd of this size, they say. That's equivalent to two hundred days' wages for the average laborer. They know they don't have that kind of money. And they know Jesus doesn't either.

For Discussion: If you had been one of the disciples that day, what would be going through your mind as you hear Jesus ordering you to give this vast crowd something to eat?

TEXT TO READ: MARK 6:38-40

COMMENT ON THE TEXT: The disciples have suggested that it would take a huge amount of money to buy food for this crowd. But they're missing the point. So Jesus asks them, "How many loaves of bread do you have? Check and see."

The disciples come back and say that they've found five loaves and two dried fish. They know that's not enough. They know that they'll run short if they try to use that. Their resources are inadequate. They're sure that Jesus will understand.

But instead, after hearing the disciples' report, Jesus begins telling the crowd to sit down. He has them sit "upon the green grass." This is a reminder of the compassionate care of a good shepherd—the kind of shepherd who will, according to Psalm 23, lead the sheep into "green pastures." Mark tells us that the crowd sits down "in ranks, by hundreds, and by fifties." Mark may be envisioning people sitting in rows, a hundred people across, fifty rows deep—some five thousand people. Or he may be trying to say, in an especially vivid way, that the crowd is huge.

For Discussion: How do you think the disciples felt when, after telling Jesus that their resources were grossly inadequate, nevertheless he told the people to sit down and get ready to eat?

TEXT TO READ: MARK 6:41

FIRST COMMENT ON THE TEXT: The disciples are stunned. But Jesus takes their meager bit of food, looks up to heaven, and speaks a blessing.

It's easy to misread this and think that Jesus is blessing the food, because that's what we in our culture would do. But in the Jewish tradition, before eating, you speak a blessing. And the blessing is on God, not on the food. You bless and praise God, who provides the food.

Such blessings are still a part of Jewish celebrations and holy days.

Often these blessings include thanksgiving for the fact that the Holy One, the Ruler of the Universe, "provides food for all." The blessing is a reminder that in God's world, no one is to go hungry. Food is given to be shared. The food provided by God is "for all God's creatures."

After blessing God and reminding his hearers of how food is not just for the rich and the powerful and not just for those who attend birthday banquets, Jesus breaks the loaves. The loaves are likely flat, chewy bread, somewhat like the pita bread that is sold today. You break off a piece to eat. So after breaking apart the loaves and the fish, Jesus hands the pieces to his disciples and tells them to take these grossly inadequate resources and use them to feed the vast crowd.

SECOND COMMENT ON THE TEXT: We can imagine the disciples rolling their eyes. We can imagine them whispering to themselves that Jesus has gone mad. We can imagine them believing that hardly anybody will have anything to eat.

They are burdened by their inadequacy. They are burdened by their shortage of resources. They are shackled by a mentality that says, "When there's not enough to go around, let everyone fend for themselves." They're forgetting that there's a God, a God who's close at hand, a God who provides food for all, as a common blessing, a common destiny.

Jesus is saying to his disciples, "Pick up your inadequacy. Take up your shortage of resources. Don't let it shackle you. Take it up, and do what you know needs to be done. Take it up, and share what you've been given. Take it up, and follow in God's way."

THIRD COMMENT ON THE TEXT: Throughout the Gospel of Mark, Jesus urges people not to be burdened by those things that seem to hold them back. He tells a paralyzed man to take up his bed and walk. He tells the disciples in a boat in the middle of a storm to take up their fears and follow in the way that God has set. And when he visits Nazareth, through his behavior, Jesus shows his disciples the importance of picking up slurs that are uttered and names that are called.

Now, here on a grassy hillside in the Galilean countryside, he's calling his disciples to take up their inadequacies, their shortage of resources, even their desire to protect what they have. He's telling them to pick up that burden, to not let it hold them back from doing what God would have them do. He wants to see them breaking free.

For too long, the rich and powerful have hogged all the resources for themselves. For too long, those who attended Herod's birthday banquet have enjoyed the fatted lamb while the weak and the poor have gone hungry. That's why it's time for the disciples to buy into a new mentality: a spirit of sharing, a spirit of common destiny, a spirit of compassion and grace toward "sheep not having a shepherd."

For Discussion: In what ways are we likewise burdened by a sense of inadequacy, a sense of shortage, a desire to protect what we have for ourselves? How can we, like the disciples, learn to take up that burden and move forward in faith?

TEXT TO READ: MARK 6:42-43

FIRST COMMENT ON THE TEXT: What a shock this must have been for the disciples! Jesus breaks the five loaves and two fish that they have, and he tells them to hand it out to the crowd that's gathered. Nervously the disciples begin passing the food around—and to their amazement, everyone eats. Everyone is filled. Then, when it's all over, they pass baskets to collect the leftovers. And each of the twelve disciples ends up with a basket. Not an empty basket. But a full basket.

For Discussion: What sort of message must the disciples have gotten that evening as they stood there on the hillside, each of them with a full basket of leftovers in his hands?

SECOND COMMENT ON THE TEXT: As it turns out, this story in Mark is remarkably similar to something that happened much earlier to the prophet Elisha. The story is told in 2 Kings 4, and it's probably a story that most devout Jews in Mark's day would know well.

The events in 2 Kings take place at a time when there is a great famine in the land. Elisha and his disciples don't have much to eat, but neither do the poor, who are struggling to survive. One day, according to 2 Kings 4, a man came to Elisha, bringing food to the man of God: twenty loaves of barley and some fresh ears of grain (2 Kings 4:42). This is a special offering for God's prophet, an exclusive gift at a time of great hardship.

Elisha's household must have been thrilled. Someone has brought them something to eat! Just as they're about to bite in, Elisha turns to his servant and says, "Give it to the people, and let them eat." Elisha's words are very similar to what Jesus tells his disciples in today's passage: "Look at these people in need. Give them something to eat."

On hearing this, Elisha's servant says, "This isn't enough! We can't share this little bit! Why, it wouldn't even feed a hundred people!" Elisha refuses to give in. He repeats his instructions, telling his servant, "Give it to the people, and let them eat, for thus says the LORD, 'They shall eat and have some left' " (2 Kings 4:43, NRSV).

So the servant takes the desperately needed food—the food that seems too little, the resources that seem too short, the nourishment that seems inadequate for the many who are hungry—and sets the food before the people and invites them to eat. They eat. And not only are they all well filled, but also there is food left over (2 Kings 4:44).

The resources that appear too little turn out to be more than enough. When a shortage of resources is used in God's way, the cupboard is never bare. The well never runs dry.

For Discussion: When Mark put his Gospel together and when he placed this story, with all its dramatic prophetic connections, right after the story of Herod's birthday banquet, what do you think he had in mind? What are the main points that you think he intended to make?

TEXT TO READ: MARK 6:44

COMMENT ON THE TEXT: The story of the feeding of the five thousand is told in Mark without any special fanfare. There's no sign that the crowd even saw it as a miracle.

What they saw was Jesus, the compassionate shepherd, linking his destiny with theirs. What they saw was Jesus, inviting them to lounge expectantly with him on the grass. What they saw was Jesus, picking up some food, looking up to heaven, and blessing the God who provides food for all. What they saw was Jesus, ordering his disciples to take what little they had and share it with those who were in need.

What they saw was that when they linked their destinies, when they responded in faith, when they threw off the shortage mentality, all their needs would be met. What they saw was that when we "break bread together on our knees" . . . when we no longer fend for ourselves but pursue the common good . . . when we move forward together in faith . . . then inadequacy becomes abundance and private shortages become common extravagances with baskets and baskets left over.

SESSION 5

AND HE WENT UP UNTO
THEM INTO THE SHIP; AND
THE WIND CEASED: AND THEY
WERE SORE AMAZED . . . AND
WONDERED. FOR THEY
CONSIDERED NOT THE
MIRACLE OF THE LOAVES . . .
—MARK 6:51-52

COME BY HERE, MY LORD

MARK 6:42-56

SETTING THE STAGE

PART ONE: Jesus and his disciples are out on a hillside. A huge crowd has come to hear Jesus' teaching. When Jesus sees them, he has compassion on them, for he sees that they are like sheep without a shepherd. Instead of feeding them, their leaders have been exploiting them. Instead of caring for them, their leaders have been abusing them. Again and again, like sheep without a shepherd, they have had to fend for themselves.

So when mid to late afternoon rolls around, the time when most Jews would eat their main meal of the day, Jesus tells his disciples to feed the crowd. They are shocked. All they have is a few loaves of bread and a couple of dried fish. They tell Jesus it isn't enough.

PART TWO: The disciples are burdened down with the mentality of shortage and frugality. But Jesus is liberated. He has a mentality of sharing. And he knows that God's intent has always been to provide food for all. So he sits these sheep down on "green pastures," right there on the hillside. And he tells them to get ready to eat.

Jesus then tells his disciples to take what seems to be too little and pass it among the people, for in reality it is more than enough. Jesus knows that when you are walking with God, when you are doing what God would have you to do, there is always enough to share with those who are in need. And the result of that sharing can be remarkable . . .

TEXT TO READ: MARK 6:42-44

COMMENT ON THE TEXT: The disciples have been paralyzed with fear. They fear there isn't enough. So they plan to hoard what little they have for themselves. But their fears turn out to be groundless. Before passing out the food, Jesus blesses God. He blesses the God who is traditionally described in Jewish prayers as One who "provides food for all." And when the food is passed, it's more than enough. Everyone eats and is filled. In fact, each of the twelve disciples gathers up a full basket of leftovers. It's incredible.

TEXT TO READ: MARK 6:45

COMMENT ON THE TEXT: The disciples are still standing there, stunned. Each is holding a full basket of leftovers. The too little has become too much. But then, "immediately," Jesus has the disciples get into a boat. He tells them to go on ahead of him, over to "the other side" of the sea, over to the city of Bethsaida.

The original Greek text emphasizes how quickly after the feeding Jesus tells the disciples to leave. "Immediately," just as soon as they have gathered the leftovers, he tells them to get out of there.

And it's not just that Jesus politely asks the disciples to go on ahead. The Greek word that is used implies that Jesus forces the disciples to go. He compels them. They have no choice. "Go," he says, "get in the boat. Go by yourselves over to the far side of the sea. Go to that territory where Jews are fewer in number. Go to that place with which you are not familiar. Go to Bethsaida, with its Gentiles and foreigners. Go, right now, as evening approaches, as night is falling. Don't delay. Go."

For Discussion: What do you suppose Jesus is up to? Why do you think he immediately orders his disciples to leave after the great feeding on the hillside? What do you think happens to the twelve baskets of food? What do you think might have been going through the disciples' minds as they head toward their boat? Are there previous experiences they might be thinking of? What happened the last time they tried to take a boat to the other side of the sea? And the last time they got to the other side of the sea, what kind of person did they run into (Mark 5:1-20)?

TEXT TO READ: MARK 6:46

COMMENT ON THE TEXT: The disciples head down to the sea. They busy themselves with the boat. They check it over, making sure everything is in order. Meanwhile Jesus dismisses the crowd. Like a good shepherd, he gently sends the crowd away. He sends them home to their towns and villages. He offers some parting words and seeks to strengthen their faith.

Then Jesus goes up on a mountain or hillside to pray. There's Someone he wants to talk with. There's Someone he needs to listen to. There's Someone whose presence he longs to be in. We don't know what Jesus prays. But Jesus is a Jew, a very devout Jew. And Jews often use the Psalms as their prayer book. So it's possible that in his prayers, Jesus recites a psalm.

And if it is a psalm that he uses as his prayer, then we can't help but wonder if the psalm might not be Psalm 107, whose words fit perfectly with that which has just happened.

BACKGROUND TEXT TO READ: PSALM 107:1-9

COMMENT ON THE TEXT: From the beginning, the Gospel of Mark has told us that the message of Jesus is that God and God's kingdom are close at hand. There is thus no need for fear. God's people are on a journey—a journey of faith. The journey will be easy. And the journey will be joyful. For it's a journey with God, who is close at hand.

With God at our side, we can pick up our burdens. We can take up those things that would hold us back. We can move forward in faith. For we don't move down this way alone. We have a graceful and merciful God close at hand, a God who is stronger and mightier than any foe.

For Jesus and for the Gospel of Mark, the feeding of five thousand on a hillside overlooking the sea is another demonstration of the truth: God is close at hand. Psalm 107 has been shown to be true. Because God is close, even when we have too little, we have too much. How can there be any doubt? God is at work. God's kingdom is close. A way is being made in the wilderness. We can move forward in faith.

TEXT TO READ: MARK 6:47-48

FIRST COMMENT ON THE TEXT: Evening comes. Darkness falls. The disciples are together, out on the Sea of Galilee. Jesus is alone, back on land, praising God for God's wonderful works. He's thanking God for filling the hungry with good things. He's blessing God for making a way through the wilderness. Psalm 107 calls on the redeemed of the Lord to say so. And Jesus is saying so.

But then, somehow, Jesus sees his disciples out on the water, out in the boat. It's not clear how he sees them. It's dark. It's night. But maybe from a hillside overlooking the sea, he catches a glimpse of them through the moonlight. Or perhaps he's given a vision of them. Perhaps it's a supernatural sensing.

In any case, he sees his disciples, straining at the oars of their boat. They're battling a fierce wind, a wind that keeps blowing them back to shore. The Greek word for the disciples' agony is vivid. Literally Mark says that the disciples are "tormented" by the wind. It's blowing directly against them, and they're having a terrible time getting anywhere.

SECOND COMMENT ON THE TEXT: By this time, most of the night has passed. The King James Version calls it "the fourth watch of the night." That falls between three and six in the morning. If the disciples have been rowing all night, they are likely exhausted. Their strength may be failing.

So Jesus, in his compassion, decides to encourage them. He wants to remind them that God's kingdom is close. He wants them to reach out and take hold of the way of faith.

If God could take their too little food and feed five thousand, then surely God can take their too little strength and get them to the other side of the sea—if only they will reach out and grab hold of God's unchanging hand!

THIRD COMMENT ON THE TEXT: Jesus has no boat. And the disciples are far out on the water. But water is no hindrance to God. In describing the great deeds of God, Psalm 77:19 says, "Your way was through the sea, your path through the mighty waters; yet your footprints were unseen" (NRSV).

The disciples see Jesus as a prophet and teacher. But Mark wants us to see Jesus as far more than that. Yes, he's a man of Galilee. Yes, he has family in Nazareth. Yes, he's a human being, just like us. But he's more than that, for through Jesus, in some special and remarkable way, God has come close. Very close. The disciples haven't yet much understood it. But in Jesus, they have God's beloved walking with them.

To comfort and strengthen his disciples, Jesus sets off through the night toward the boat where the disciples struggle against the wind. He has no boat to carry him. So he walks. He walks on the water, empowered by the One who has made the sea, empowered by the One whose path is "through the mighty waters" (Psalm 77:19, NRSV).

For Discussion: Jesus wants to encourage his weary disciples, who are out there on the sea, tormented with a wind that is blowing in the wrong direction. He wants to build up their confidence and their commitment to pushing on in the way of faith. But how is he planning to do that? What do you think the text means when it says that he intends to pass them by?

FOURTH COMMENT ON THE TEXT: In the Hebrew Scriptures, when God wants to encourage and strengthen a weary people, it's sometimes said that God passes by them.

God is too holy to be seen. God is too mighty to encounter face-to-face. But sometimes, when God's people are discouraged or when they need a sense of direction, the Hebrew Scriptures talk about God's spirit passing by them.

Once, when Moses is feeling weary, when Moses is feeling like his strength is too little, when Moses is doubting that God is still close, God takes Moses and hides him "in the cleft of a rock," and while Moses stands there, God's glory "passed by" (Exodus 33:22, NRSV).

Later, the prophet Elijah also becomes discouraged. He's not battling a wind, like the disciples. But he's battling a great wickedness throughout the land. He feels alone. He feels defeated. His strength seems to be too little for the task to which God has called him. Elijah turns to God in despair. He cries out to God, saying, "The Israelites have forsaken your covenant, thrown down your altars, and killed your prophets with the

sword. I alone am left, and they are seeking my life, to take it away."
Then Elijah is told, "Go out and stand on the mountain before the LORD,
for the LORD is about to pass by" (1 Kings 19:10-11, NRSV).

So perhaps what Jesus intends to do, early that morning, in the darkness on the Sea of Galilee, is to pass by his disciples. Perhaps what he intends to do is to remind them, as he has so often, that God is close at hand. Perhaps what he intends to do is to give them a glimpse of God's Spirit, rowing with them across the sea, standing with them against the wind, pulling with them on the oars.

For Discussion: The Bible says no one has ever seen God, but in what kinds of situations have you perhaps felt God's presence passing by in a special sort of way? What was the effect of this experience?

FIFTH COMMENT ON THE TEXT: During a sermon at Ebenezer Baptist Church in Atlanta, Dr. Martin Luther King Jr. once talked about a time, after the Montgomery bus boycott, when he felt God's presence pass by in a very special way. The sermon was later included in his book *The Strength to Love*.

In his sermon, Dr. King explained that he had been immobilized by threats and middle-of-the-night phone calls. He could feel fear growing in his heart. One night, tired and afraid, he got up, made coffee, and sank into a chair with his head in his hands. Finally he prayed, explaining to God that he didn't have what it took to go on. He couldn't do it any more. He was out of strength, out of courage.

At that very moment, he said, it was as if God's presence swept through the room—in a way that he had never felt before. An inner voice seemed to reassure him that if he continued to stand up for righteousness and truth, God would be with him—with him forever.

TEXT TO READ: MARK 6:49-50

FIRST COMMENT ON THE TEXT: The disciples, out on that boat, fighting that wind, are weary and worn. They aren't sure they have the strength to continue. Like Dr. King, they are at the end of their powers. They are ready to give up.

So Jesus, in his compassion, walks out on the water. He intends to pass by them in a way that will take away their fears, in a way that will renew their faith. But when the disciples catch a glimpse of Jesus coming toward them, they are terrified. They scream in fright. You can imagine the pandemonium. Instead of being strengthened, they are plunged even further into fear. Instead of seeing the presence of God, they think they are being visited by a ghost.

SECOND COMMENT ON THE TEXT: There's such screaming and carrying on that Jesus has to abandon his original intent. He stops and speaks. The King James Version translates Jesus' first words as "Be of good cheer." But that makes for too cheery a feel. Other translations do a better job with "Take heart!" Or, "Be of good courage!"

Jesus is telling a frightened boatload of weary disciples to pull themselves together. He's telling them to stand strong—and to let courage take root in their hearts.

Then he says, "It's me. I am the one walking on the water. No ghost. No spirit from the underworld. No demon. Just me. I am the one who has come to greet you."

In the midst of the chaos on the boat, in the midst of the screaming and yelling and frantic grabbing hold of one another, Jesus speaks a word of comfort. He assures the disciples that he is the one they are seeing—and no other: "Fear not. Don't be afraid. It's me!"

For Discussion: Why do you think the disciples panic when Jesus tries to strengthen and comfort them? In what kinds of situations might we too misunderstand or misinterpret something that God does to strengthen us?

THIRD COMMENT ON THE TEXT: This scene on the Sea of Galilee is part of Mark's larger message. We see Jesus having compassion on his disciples. He sees their struggle. He understands their exhaustion. He wants to renew their faith, to rebuild their strength. These are the very qualities that Mark shows us in Jesus throughout the Gospel.

We also see Jesus passing by the boat. Thereby Jesus seeks to remind his disciples that God is nearby. It's the same message that he has been proclaiming from the beginning. "The time is fulfilled," he keeps saying. "and the kingdom of God is at hand" (Mark 1:15).

But throughout the Gospel, the disciples don't much understand. The Gospel of Mark tends to paint a negative picture of the disciples. It shows us their weakness, their fears, their misunderstandings. So when the disciples scream in terror, we aren't surprised.

TEXT TO READ: MARK 6:51-52

FIRST COMMENT ON THE TEXT: After telling his disciples to renew their courage and not be afraid, Jesus climbs into the boat with them. Immediately the wind stops. There's no indication that Jesus commands it to stop. We don't see Jesus getting up and speaking to the waves, "Peace! Be still!" No, the wind simply stops. And a calm comes over the waters.

Mark tells us that the disciples are "utterly astounded" (NRSV). They can't believe it. They have worked all night, pulling vainly on their oars, getting nowhere. Until Jesus steps into the boat, they're convinced that they have too little strength to make it. They're burdened by inadequacy. They're ready to give up. They think that they can't make it.

Then Jesus steps into the boat. He brings a heart of faith. The wind stops. The howling is no more. The disciples are stunned.

For Discussion: Mark says that the reason the disciples are so astonished is that "they did not understand about the loaves" (NRSV). What do the loaves have to do with it? What is it about the loaves that could have made a difference for the disciples that windy night on the sea?

SECOND COMMENT ON THE TEXT: Mark concludes his remarks about the disciples' astonishment by saying that "their heart was hardened." Mark never conveys a very positive picture of the disciples. Occasionally they manage to do the right thing. But more often than not, they seem to miss the point. Again and again, they behave with fear rather than with faith.

For Mark to declare that their hearts were hardened is a harsh statement. The last time that the Gospel of Mark described someone as having a hardened heart was in Mark 3:5, where a group of religious leaders criticize Jesus for healing a man on the Sabbath, and we're told that Jesus "grieved for the hardness of their hearts." Now Jesus' disciples have fallen into this same category. They too have hardened their hearts.

TEXT TO READ: MARK 6:53

COMMENT ON THE TEXT: After Jesus gets into the boat and the wind dies down, the group makes its way back to shore. They tie up their boat at Gennesaret, a little town back on the same side of the sea that they started from.

For Discussion: How do you imagine the disciples are feeling as they pull their boat up onto shore? How can we keep from having hardened hearts?

TEXT TO READ: MARK 6:54-55

FIRST COMMENT ON THE TEXT: Mark's portrait of how people respond to Jesus is interesting. First we see Jesus rejected by established religious leaders. Later we see him rejected by his family and by folks who live in his hometown. They think he's a nobody—or worse. Now, even his disciples are described as having hardened hearts. They too are closing themselves off from the message. They too are tightening up with fear. They too are letting themselves be beaten down with burdens. They too are refusing to walk in the way of faith.

But there is a group that constitutes good earth. There is a group that seems to hear and understand. There is a group that is willing to pick up its bed and walk. There is a group that is breaking free. It's the common folk. The poor folk. The sick folk. The rejected folk. Those who don't know where else to turn. Those who have waited for so long, believing that one day, God's hand will come close, just as the great Jewish prophets have said . . .

SECOND COMMENT ON THE TEXT: Those who hear and understand do so without hesitation. They are good earth, just like the good soil that Jesus describes in his parable of a farmer going out to sow seeds. They are willing to dream new dreams. They are willing to act in faith. They are willing to pick up their burdens and follow in a way of God's making. They are willing to envision new possibilities. They are willing to sit down and eat when Jesus says to do so, even if it seems like there isn't enough food on hand. They are willing to come running to Jesus from cities and towns and farms, carrying friends and loved ones if need be, setting them down before Jesus on streets and in marketplaces. They aren't governed by fear. They're governed by faith.

The contrasts here at the end of Mark 6 are startling. First, Jesus' twelve handpicked disciples say that the food that they have is too little. But five thousand people think differently and sit down anyway. They believe. Unlike the disciples, they are willing to live and act in faith.

Then we see these same handpicked disciples growing weary as they battle a wind on the sea. They are ready to give up. They say the strength that they have is too little. Jesus seeks to pass them by. He seeks to remind them of God's enduring presence. But they scream in terror.

Later these same disciples get back to land. Someone on shore recognizes Jesus. Word spreads. Soon a mob of common folk is rushing from everywhere just to be next to Jesus. They spread their mats in the highways and byways and in the marketplaces. And when Jesus passes by these common folk, they don't scream in fright. Instead they reach out in faith. They don't cry in terror. They simply sing:

Kum ba yah, my Lord, kum ba yah.
Come by here, my Lord, come by here.

Unlike the disciples, these common folk, these poor folk, these struggling folk long for Jesus to come close—for they know that even a touch of the hem of his garment will make them whole.

SESSION 6

AND HE CHARGED THEM,
SAYING, TAKE HEED, BEWARE
OF THE LEAVEN OF THE
PHARISEES, AND OF THE
LEAVEN OF HEROD.
—MARK 8:15

DO YOU STILL
NOT UNDERSTAND?

MARK 8:10-21

SETTING THE STAGE

In today's passage from the Gospel of Mark, Jesus has been traveling through Gentile territory. He has healed a Syro-Phoenician woman's daughter. He has healed a man who was deaf and mute. And he has fed a huge crowd with a handful of bread, just as he did earlier when he was in Jewish territory.

Mark has been trying to show his readers that the blessings of God are for all the world. God is gathering in the disconsolate, wherever they languish. Some are Jews. Some are Gentiles. None are superior. None are inferior. God calls from the east. God calls from the west. God calls from the north. God calls from the south. All feast at the same table.

After feeding four thousand people over on the Gentile side of the Sea of Galilee, Jesus and his disciples get into a boat and head back across the water to Jewish territory.

Many scholars feel that the verses that we look at today constitute the conclusion to the first half of the Gospel. If Mark is a drama in two acts, then these verses close the curtain on the first act in the drama.

TEXT TO READ: MARK 8:10

COMMENT ON THE TEXT: No one knows for sure where Dalmanutha is. There is no place with that name any more. But because Pharisees appear there, most scholars think Dalmanutha is back on the Jewish side of the Sea of Galilee.

TEXT TO READ: MARK 8:11

FIRST COMMENT ON THE TEXT: In Mark's fast-moving drama, Jesus and the disciples have barely gotten out of their boat when Pharisees once again pounce on Jesus "to question with him."

As a skillful storyteller, Mark likes to wrap together whole sections of his drama in special ways. He likes to wrap up loose ends and show how different parts are related. When we look at short passages in isolation, we sometimes miss what Mark is up to.

But if we were to look back over the last few chapters in Mark, we would see that the arguments of the Pharisees constitute both a beginning and an end for Jesus' journey into Gentile territories. The whole sequence of Gentile stories begins right after the dispute between Jesus and the Pharisees about what is unclean. And now, as soon as Jesus returns from his journey among the Gentiles, the Pharisees are at him again. Their attacks on him become the front cover and back cover for this whole sequence of events.

Mark doesn't want us to see these Gentile events in isolation. Rather, he wants us to see them as a powerful contrast to the us-versus-them thinking that is so typical of religious people, even today.

The Pharisees don't just argue with Jesus. Mark tells us that they begin "tempting him." In effect, they test him. They challenge him. They crank up the pressure to see if he'll crack.

For Discussion: This is the second time in the Gospel of Mark that we hear about someone tempting Jesus. Who was it the first time (Mark 1:13)? When Mark says that religious people with an excluding mentality are "tempting" Jesus, into whose camp does this put them? What does this say about religious people today who view others as unclean?

SECOND COMMENT ON THE TEXT: There's one other thing that Mark says the Pharisees are doing. Mark says that they are trying to get Jesus to give them "a sign from heaven." This would be some kind of validation that what he's saying is true. After all, he's been declaring that the kingdom of God is close at hand. He's been speaking with authority, telling people that this is a time for faith, not fear. He's been acting like a prophet. So they want him to make God offer some divine sign from heaven that will validate his testimony.

In their mind, a sign from heaven is not the same as feeding a crowd with a handful of bread. It's not the same as causing the lame to walk or the deaf to hear. It's not the same as reaching out with compassion to the poor and distressed.

The kind of sign they are demanding is some kind of specific declaration by Jesus that on such-and-such a day, God will do some very unusual thing—causing fire to erupt in the sea or turning a river into blood or causing locusts to overrun the land. It has to be announced in advance that this is what will happen. Otherwise they don't consider it a sign.

THIRD COMMENT ON THE TEXT: By asking for a sign, the Pharisees show that they do not believe that Jesus is a legitimate messenger from God.

An old spiritual talks about "waking up this morning" and having "no doubt." But the Pharisees and their modern equivalents seem to wake up every morning filled with doubt. Their hearts are like the hard earth. The seed falls, but it never penetrates the soil. Birds come and devour the seed before it has the slightest chance to produce any faith.

For Discussion: What are the ways that we too sometimes "tempt" God by demanding a sign from heaven?

TEXT TO READ: MARK 8:12

FIRST COMMENT ON THE TEXT: Mark doesn't tell us what the Pharisees are questioning Jesus about on this occasion. But they are one of the main champions of keeping Jews and Gentiles apart. They may have heard about some of the things Jesus did during his absence from Galilee. If so, they may be criticizing him for his interaction with those they consider unclean.

When they demand that Jesus produce a sign from heaven that will provide legitimacy for his outrageous behavior, we're told that "Jesus sighed deeply in his spirit." But this sigh is very different from the sigh that Jesus gave in Mark 7:34, where he creatively breathes the breath of life into a deaf and mute man.

There are several reasons for believing that this is a different kind of sigh. For one thing, there's no work of creation here. For another, when Jesus sighs and heals the deaf and mute man, he begins by "looking up to heaven." That connects his sigh there with the work of the divine Creator. But here he is sighing "in his spirit." This is more like an internal sigh of despair.

As it turns out, the Greek word used in Mark 7:34 is different from the Greek word used in Mark 8:12. So it seems likely that Mark intends the two words to be understood differently. In many English translations, both words get translated as "sigh." So we don't realize that in the original Greek, they're slightly different words, each with its own connotation.

SECOND COMMENT ON THE TEXT: The Greek word for a despairing sigh, the word that's used in Mark 8:12, is used in only a few other parts of Scripture. And Mark may be thinking of one of these passages when he paints for us this scene with Jesus and the Pharisees.

Perhaps the most memorable place in all of Scripture where this Greek word appears is in the Book of Susanna. Many of us aren't familiar with the Book of Susanna because it's not in most Bibles used by Protestants. Instead, it's found in what's called the Apocrypha.

But Susanna is a part of the Scriptures that Jesus would have used. And it's a part of the Scriptures that the writer of Mark would have known. The first readers of the Gospel would also have known it well because the story of Susanna is dramatic and memorable.

THIRD COMMENT ON THE TEXT: According to the Book of Susanna, Susanna is a beautiful young woman living in the land of Babylon. She is a Jew. Her parents are righteous, and they have taught her the ways of faith. So she fears the Lord. And she always tries to do what is right.

As it happens, two elders are appointed to provide moral leadership for the Jewish community. But like too many religious leaders throughout history, these elders are wicked. Their hearts are corrupt. And they begin to lust after Susanna.

One day, these two corrupt elders hide in the garden behind Susanna's house, and before long, Susanna comes out to bathe. When her maids leave and she is alone in the garden, the wicked elders burst out from their hiding place and say to her, "Look, the garden doors are shut, and no one can see us. We are burning with desire for you. So give your consent and lie with us—or we will testify falsely against you and tell people that a young man was with you and this is why you sent your maids away" (vv. 20-21).

FOURTH COMMENT ON THE TEXT: Like the scribes and Pharisees will eventually do with Jesus, these corrupt elders threaten to testify falsely against Susanna. Like the scribes and Pharisees, they seek to trap her. They are tempting her, in the sense of putting her to the test, just like the scribes and Pharisees do with Jesus.

When Susanna sees the situation, the text of the book says, she sighs deeply within her, and the word that's used is the same Greek word that Mark uses to describe Jesus when he is questioned by the Pharisees.

Susanna realizes she has been trapped by people who should be people of God but who are instead working for evil. But Susanna is a woman of faith, and despite the intolerable situation, she refuses their demands, refusing to "sin in the sight of the Lord." The wicked leaders then fulfill their promise. Immediately they testify against her, and their false testimony results in Susanna being sentenced to death, just as Jesus will be.

FIFTH COMMENT ON THE TEXT: So when Mark uses this same word to describe Jesus as "sighing deeply in his spirit" at the demands the Pharisees make of him, it seems likely that Mark is remembering the apocryphal story of Susanna.

Through Jesus' despairing sigh, Mark is indicating to us, his readers, where the story of Jesus is headed. Jesus, like Susanna, will be the victim of false testimony. Jesus, like Susanna, will be the victim of corrupt religious leaders out to satisfy their own evil desires. And Jesus, like Susanna, will be sentenced to death—not for something wrong that he has done but for standing up for God and God's ways.

The despairing sigh of Jesus in Mark 8:12 is an ominous sign. It foreshadows the future by reminding us of the similarity between the stories of Jesus and Susanna.

For Discussion: What have been some of those times when you have felt trapped between impossible options, times when you felt like giving a despairing sigh? How do we find the strength, like Jesus and Susanna, to choose what is right, even in such situations?

SIXTH COMMENT ON THE TEXT: After giving a despairing sigh, Jesus wonders aloud why "this generation" seeks after a sign from heaven. The implication of Jesus' words is that no further sign is needed. Everything is clear. All needed signs have already been given. The deaf hear. The hungry eat. The weak are made strong. The poor are filled. The lame walk. God's call is being heard by Jews and Gentiles alike. Faith is growing. Too little has become too much. No more fasting. The feasting has begun. For as it says in Mark 1:15, the time is fulfilled. The kingdom of God is close at hand. What further sign could be needed?

The generation that God brought out of Egypt, the generation that moved from slavery to freedom—they too sometimes demanded a sign. In the wilderness wanderings, on the way to the Promised Land, they would begin to doubt. They would forget all that had happened. Their eyes would be closed to what God was doing in their midst, day after day, night after night. So the attitude that Jesus encounters among the people of his generation is nothing new.

SEVENTH COMMENT ON THE TEXT: Psalm 95 talks about that time when the generation that left Egypt demanded a sign. And Psalm 95 warns the people of God not to be like that generation. Here's part of what the psalm says, speaking, as it were, for God: "Do not harden your hearts, as at Meribah, as on the day at Massah in the wilderness, when your ancestors tested me, and put me to the proof, though they had seen my work" (Psalm 95:8-9, NRSV).

Meribah and Massah are two of the wilderness places where the people of Israel tested and tempted God by demanding a sign, even though they "had seen my work." The way that Jesus responds to the Pharisees' demand for a sign puts the Pharisees in the same camp as those foolish people who had been brought from slavery but then forgot the power and glory of God.

Psalm 95 goes on to say that for forty years, God "loathed that generation and said, 'They are a people whose hearts go astray' " (Psalm 95:10, NRSV). So when Jesus says "no sign will be given unto this generation," he is saying that the Pharisees are like the generation that came from Egypt and was blind to the work of God in their midst. Jesus is saying that the work of God is all around you. No further sign is needed, for the truth is evident for all who are willing to see it.

TEXT TO READ: MARK 8:13

COMMENT ON THE TEXT: After declaring to the Pharisees that no sign will be given to the likes of them, Jesus turns around. This is one of the few places in the whole Gospel where Jesus deliberately leaves someone. And here he not only turns around and leaves the Pharisees standing there, but also he gets back into a boat and once again crosses over to "the other side."

He goes again to the far side of the Sea of Galilee. He leaves behind not only the Pharisees but also their area of influence. He goes over again to the Gentile side of the sea, as if to say to the Pharisees, "Those people that you think are so far from God are a lot closer to God than you folks who keep trying to exclude them. They see the signs. Their hearts are open. And it is in them, not in you, that I have found fertile soil."

TEXT TO READ: MARK 8:14

COMMENT ON THE TEXT: At first glance, this verse seems contradictory. First we learn that the disciples haven't remembered to bring any bread with them. Then we're told that they did have one loaf with them. How can they have "no bread" and "one loaf"?

Part of the confusion is the way the text is translated. In English, there's no plural for "bread." The word *bread* can mean one loaf, two loaves, ten loaves, or a hundred loaves. The Greek text of Mark is more specific. Literally it says that the disciples have forgotten to bring "loaves" (plural)—for all they have with them in the boat is "one loaf" (singular).

In other words, they meant to bring a supply of bread with them, but in their haste to get to the boat after Jesus' discouraging encounter with the Pharisees, they forgot. All they have with them is a single loaf of bread. And that single loaf will now become part of Jesus' lesson to them.

TEXT TO READ: MARK 8:15

COMMENT ON THE TEXT: While Jesus and the disciples are crossing the Sea of Galilee, the disciples are worrying about the fact that they have only one loaf of bread. But Jesus is still pondering his encounter with the Pharisees. He's realizing how dangerous their viewpoint is. So after a while, he looks at the disciples and he says, "Beware! Watch out for the leaven of the Pharisees—and the leaven of Herod! Don't let their way of thinking get hold of your heart! Don't let it work its way into your mind!"

In talking about the viewpoint of the Pharisees and Herod, Jesus uses the word *leaven*. That's another word for "yeast." It's what gets into bread and makes it rise. It takes over. It grows. And it consumes everything in its path.

The Pharisees oppose any interaction between Jews and Gentiles. They are separatists. They look down on Gentiles and want to keep them in a second-class status. Maintaining the separation works to the Pharisees' advantage, because it ensures their place in society.

Herod and his political cronies want to bring Jews and Gentiles together for their own political gain. Rome finds the intricate social rules a hassle. The lands around Palestine could be combined and controlled better if everyone was forced into a single culture. Unlike Jesus, who wants to bring everyone to the liberating feast of God, Herod and his cronies want to bring everyone together so that they can be oppressed more easily and so that their individual cultures and identities can be wiped out. For Herod and his cronies, it is a matter of political control.

For Discussion: What viewpoints in our society remind you of either the attitude of the Pharisees or the attitude of Herod? Who do religious people today try to exclude or treat as second class? What do you think Mark would say about this? In what ways do our modern viewpoints act like yeast, consuming the individuals who hold them?

TEXT TO READ: MARK 8:16

COMMENT ON THE TEXT: The disciples can be pretty dim-witted sometimes. So when Jesus tells them to watch out for the leaven of the Pharisees and the leaven of Herod, they think he's talking about the fact that they have brought along no loaves (plural) and all they have is one loaf of bread. They think Jesus is saying that they should be careful not to buy more bread from the Pharisees or from Herod and his pals.

The disciples make the mistake of taking Jesus literally. They forget that sometimes people use figures of speech. In his parables and in his teaching, Jesus often uses imagery. But the disciples forget that. So they think he's criticizing them for bringing only one loaf of bread. They don't understand what he's trying to say.

For Discussion: Why is it that some people, even in our day, insist on taking every verse in the Bible literally? Why is it that they have so little understanding of poetry, figurative language, or the multiple layers of meaning in Jesus' parables? How can we learn to listen more carefully to what the Bible means and not just what it seems to say on the surface?

TEXT TO READ: MARK 8:17-18

COMMENT ON THE TEXT: Jesus hears the disciples talking about his comment. And he realizes that they think he is talking about the fact that they only have one loaf of bread among them. He's dumbfounded. He can't believe it. "Don't you understand anything?" he asks. "Is your heart hard? Are your eyes closed? Are your ears plugged? What's going on?"

In asking about their heart and their eyes and their ears, Jesus is asking about the same parts of the body that are mentioned in Deuteronomy 29:2-4, when Moses has gathered the people of Israel together to present his final comments before they go on to enter the Promised Land. In those verses, Moses says to the people, "You have seen all that the LORD did before your eyes in the land of Egypt, to Pharaoh and to all his servants . . . signs and those great wonders. But to this day the LORD has not given you a mind to understand [a heart to know], or eyes to see, or ears to hear" (NRSV).

Like so many of us, the disciples are slow to understand. This first half of the Gospel has been filled with signs and wonders. It's been as clear as it could be that the day of the Lord is at hand. God is at work, not just among Jews but also among Gentiles. Satan is being bound. Faith is making a way out of no way, bringing together all who hear God's call. But the disciples haven't yet understood. Their hearts are still hard. Their eyes are still closed. Their ears are still plugged. They aren't yet breaking free.

TEXT TO READ: MARK 8:19-20

COMMENT ON THE TEXT: To make his point more vividly, Jesus now asks his disciples to remember two specific incidents. And he not only asks them to remember but also quizzes them about these events. He wants these happenings to be as vivid in their minds as possible.

First he recalls the feeding of the five thousand people, most of them Jews. "When I took five loaves and fed five thousand," he asks, "how many baskets of leftovers did you pick up?" They answer twelve.

Then he recalls the feeding of the four thousand people, most of them Gentiles, drawn from the four corners of the earth: from the east and the west, from the north and the south. "When I took seven loaves and fed four thousand," he asks, "how many baskets of leftovers did you pick up?" They answer seven.

In our English translations, both questions sound similar, for in both cases Jesus asks the disciples how many baskets they picked up. But in the original Greek, the two questions are a bit different. The word used for "baskets" in the first question is different from the word used in the second question. The kind of basket referred to in the first question is distinctly Jewish in style. And the kind of basket referred to in the second question is distinctly Gentile in style.

So by his questions, Jesus is reminding the disciples of the two kinds of people that have been fed. He is reminding them that in both cases, too little became more than enough.

For Discussion: What do you think Jesus is trying to do by reminding the disciples about these two feedings? What are they supposed to understand from Jesus' questions?

TEXT TO READ: MARK 8:21

COMMENT ON THE TEXT: After reminding the disciples about the two feedings—a feast for the Jews and a feast for the Gentiles—he leaves them with a penetrating question. "How is it," he asks, "that you still do not understand?" And with those haunting words echoing in their ears, the disciples finish their journey across the sea.

And with this question, Mark closes the first act in his Gospel drama. So the question is for us as well. Do we understand the meaning of what's happened in the story so far? Have we let it penetrate our souls? Mark is asking us too to examine our lives. Are our lives still consumed by the mentality of arrogance, oppression, pride, and fear? Instead of following in the way of God, have we let the leaven of the Pharisees or the leaven of Herod consume our souls?

In this first half of Mark, we've seen a Jesus who has a vision about God and God's way in the world. Like Ezekiel, who according to an old spiritual "saw the wheel, way up in the middle of the air," Jesus sees "a big wheel run by faith, and a little wheel run by the grace of God—a wheel in a wheel way up in the middle of the air." The wheel in a wheel isn't just spinning for one narrow group of people. It's spinning for all who will take up their bed and walk. It's spinning for all who will reach out and touch the hem of Jesus' garment. It's spinning for all who are hungry and longing for something to eat. It's spinning for all who are deaf and longing to hear. It's a wheel of faith and a wheel of grace, intertwined and interlocked.

But as one verse of an old spiritual says:

> Ol' Satan wears a clubfoot shoe,
> an' if you don' min', he'll slip it on you.

Like Jesus' closest disciples, even we who hear and understand need to be on guard for the leaven of the Pharisees and the leaven of Herod. If we aren't careful, Satan will slip his clubfoot shoe on our feet—and keep us from walking in the way of faith.

"How is it," Jesus asks, "that you still do not understand? How is it that you are not yet breaking free?"

SESSION 7

. . . AND BY THE WAY
HE ASKED HIS DISCIPLES,
SAYING UNTO THEM,
WHOM DO MEN SAY
THAT I AM?
—MARK 8:27

A NEW WAY FOR US ALL

MARK 8:27-32A

SETTING THE STAGE

In the central portion of his Gospel, Mark questions how well we understand who Jesus is and how well we are walking in the new way that God is making. Mark seems to be suggesting that our first impressions may not be right. Even when Jesus has gently touched us, we, like the disciples, may still be lacking in understanding. We may still see incorrectly. Like the blind man, after that first touch from Jesus, we may see only partially. We may catch a glimmer of the truth but find it distorted.

Mark wants us to break through the fog. He wants us to see clearly. He wants to challenge the broken and distorted understandings that can so easily creep into our souls. Today's verses from Mark continue that process.

TEXT TO READ: MARK 8:27

FIRST COMMENT ON THE TEXT: Caesarea Philippi is a major Roman city north of Galilee. It's farther north than anywhere that Mark, until now, has shown Jesus going. Not only is it a city with a strong Roman presence, but it is also a city connected with the worship of false gods. Centuries before the time of Jesus, people came here to worship Baal. Later a grotto was built to honor the Greek god Pan.

At the time of Jesus, the city has been rebuilt by Herod Philip. He is one of the small-time kings installed by Rome to rule its territory. Herod Philip has renamed the city Caesarea Philippi. The Caesarea part is in honor of the Roman caesar. And Philippi is in honor of himself. So, by its very name, the city of Caesarea Philippi shows that it bows to Rome and to those whom Rome has installed to rule and oppress the people.

If that isn't enough, Herod the Great, the murderer of John the Baptist, has also gone into Caesarea Philippi and built a temple in honor of the Roman ruler Caesar Augustus. Rome's rulers see themselves as gods, and they want to be worshiped as such.

SECOND COMMENT ON THE TEXT: When Jesus and the disciples go into the villages surrounding Caesarea Philippi, they are taking themselves into territory that any spiritually or politically sensitive Jew would find deeply repulsive. From both a political and spiritual viewpoint, Caesarea Philippi symbolizes the deepest evils of Mark's day.

For Jesus and his disciples to go to Caesarea Philippi is a bit like having a group of freedom-loving Africans, during slave days, go to visit the outskirts of a major fort that has been built by slave traders, inside of which is a religious temple where these slave traders and their armed guards bow in worship to themselves.

As we consider the story that begins with this verse, we need to remember what a deeply offensive and repulsive place Caesarea Philippi is to Jesus and his disciples.

For Discussion: What effect do you think it had on the disciples to go to such a place? What kinds of places for us might be similar to Caesarea Philippi, places spiritually and politically offensive? What emotions would we feel if we went to such a place?

THIRD COMMENT ON THE TEXT: Jesus and the disciples are visiting the small towns and villages around the city of Caesarea Philippi. They're visiting people living in the shadows of an evil fortress. These people know its terrors firsthand. These people, if they have any degree of sensitivity, tremble at what they see and hear around them.

As Jesus and the disciples go to and fro in the region of Caesarea Philippi, Jesus asks his disciples, "Who do people say I am?" He wants to know what the disciples have heard folk saying. He wants to know who folk think he is.

He's not asking if they know that his name is Jesus. He's not asking if they know that he's from Nazareth. Rather, he wants to know what role they think he's playing. He wants to know how they interpret the things he is saying and doing. When they see him, do they see who he really is? Or do they see him through a fog, as if he's a tree, walking around on its roots?

FOURTH COMMENT ON THE TEXT: Mark is a writer. He chooses his words carefully. And he loves to use words and phrases that make connections to other things. So sometimes he gives his drama extra layers of meaning by using words and phrases that carry symbolic significance.

At first it might seem unimportant to us that it is while Jesus and the disciples are on "the way" between villages that Jesus asks them whom people say he is. But even this simple phrase—on "the way"—has an extra layer of meaning.

On one level, when Mark says they are on the way, he means that Jesus and the disciples are walking between towns. But "the way" is a special phrase that appears many times in Mark. And it's possible that Mark wants those of us who read his Gospel to picture Jesus and the disciples as being on the way in another sense as well.

BACKGROUND TEXT TO READ: MARK 1:1-3

For Discussion: From these opening verses of the Gospel, what do we learn about the extra layer of meaning that Mark puts on "the way"? What additional significance does that extra layer of meaning bring to the verse we read in Mark 8:27, where Jesus and the disciples are said to be on the way?

TEXT TO READ: MARK 8:28

For Discussion: The disciples answer Jesus' question by mentioning John the Baptist and Elijah and "one of the prophets." In what scene in Mark are these same three explanations of Jesus offered (Mark 6:14-15)?

What gruesome story came immediately after (Mark 6:16-28)? What do you think Mark might be doing for the reader by repeating those explanations here?

TEXT TO READ: MARK 8:29A

COMMENT ON THE TEXT: In Mark's vivid drama, the disciples are on edge. They've been trying to walk with Jesus on the way. Without really knowing where they're headed, they've been walking with Jesus on the new way that God has been making through the wilderness.

But that new way has taken them past vivid reminders of Roman power. It's taken them to the region of Caesarea Philippi, with its idolatrous temples to the principalities and powers. Deep within, they can feel the fears and longings of those they meet. Their strength fades. They feel so small. What are they in relation to the monster that is Rome? Socially, spiritually, politically, and economically, they don't know where to turn.

Jesus hopes that by now the disciples fully understand what God's new way is like. But he's afraid they've missed it. He's afraid they might be seeing the world through foggy lenses. So after asking about what other people say, he turns the question on them. "But whom say ye that I am?" he asks. He wants to know if they understand. He wants to know if their eyes are open. He wants to know if their hearts are ready.

Mark uses Jesus' question as a way of advancing the drama. But he also uses it as a way of addressing us, his readers. Who do we say Jesus is? Do we understand what God is doing?

TEXT TO READ: MARK 8:29B

COMMENT ON THE TEXT: Immediately Peter answers Jesus' question. He blurts out his answer. "You are the Christ," he says. "You are our messiah!"

At this point, most of us who read Mark's Gospel are ready to rejoice. Finally, we think, Peter has it right. Finally the disciples understand. Finally the fog is lifting. Finally they're getting the picture. After all, isn't Jesus the Christ? Isn't that what Mark's Gospel is about?

Prior to this pronouncement from Peter, the word *Christ* has appeared only once in Mark's Gospel, and that's in chapter 1, verse 1, where Mark writes, "The beginning of the gospel of Jesus Christ." From the beginning of his book, Mark has clued us in. From the beginning, we are expecting, anticipating, waiting for this word from Peter: "You are the Christ!"

But just when we are rejoicing with Peter on his insight, Mark surprises us. He turns the tables. And suddenly we aren't so sure that either Peter—or we—know what we're talking about. Suddenly Mark challenges us to think again, to think more deeply, lest we see Jesus as a tree, walking around on its roots.

TEXT TO READ: MARK 8:30

For Discussion: Why do you think Jesus immediately turns on the disciples and orders them to tell their interpretation to no one? Why doesn't Jesus praise Peter for his insight? Why doesn't Jesus urge the disciples to go out and be a witness? What is it about Peter's answer that disturbs Jesus? What's going on here?

FIRST COMMENT ON THE TEXT: The Greek word that Mark uses to describe Jesus' response is extremely intense. The King James Version translates it by saying that Jesus "charged" the disciples to tell no one that he is the Christ. The New Revised Standard Version says that Jesus "sternly ordered" the disciples to tell no one.

This is the same word that Mark uses to describe Jesus' firm command to demons (Mark 1:25; 3:12). And it's the same word that Mark uses to describe Jesus ordering the winds and the waves to stop their storming. It's a word that expresses deep determination. It's a command given with authority and power. It's a command given to demons that serve the wrong master. And it's a command given to the wind and waves when they blow in the wrong direction.

So when Mark uses the same word here, we know that Jesus is not making a mild request. This is a stern command, and it is given not just to Peter but to all the disciples. Under no circumstances are they to tell anyone that he is the messiah. That is the wrong message. By itself, that is the wrong understanding. If they were to tell that to others, they would be spreading falsehood rather than truth.

The portrait that Mark gives us is a portrait of a man steeped in humility. He doesn't seek fancy titles for himself. He doesn't seek status or prestige. He doesn't want his disciples to repeat words that others might misunderstand. Rather, Mark's Jesus prefers the approach that is expressed in an old gospel song, where it says, "May the works I do speak for me."

SECOND COMMENT ON THE TEXT: Over the centuries, Jewish believers often longed for a messiah. But at different times and in different places, there were widely differing ideas about who that messiah would be and what role that messiah would play.

Jesus' day is a time of great oppression. All of Palestine is under the harsh and greedy thumb of Rome. And as is so often the case, the dominant political power has also tried to become the dominant spiritual power. Even religious leaders are falling under Roman sway. And Caesarea Philippi, where Jesus and his disciples have been traveling, is a vivid reminder of that.

In such a context, it was natural for Jews to long for a messiah. They longed for someone who would rise up with military power against Roman oppression. They longed for someone who would raise an army, engage in battle, slaughter thousands, and come out a victor. They dreamed of an iron-fisted messiah who would rule as king over all of the Jewish people.

But their visions were clouded in fog. It was like looking at people and seeing trees, walking about on their roots. People aren't trees. And the messiah they longed for wasn't the messiah God was sending.

They were thinking in old ways. Fruitless ways. They had misunderstood the words of the prophets. They were forgetting that God had promised to make a new way through the wilderness. In that new way, swords would be beaten into plowshares. In that new way, grace and justice would flow like mighty, rushing streams. In that new way, all people, even the weakest and the most powerless, would feel loved and embraced.

THIRD COMMENT ON THE TEXT: Jesus and the disciples have been traveling in the region around Caesarea Philippi, a shameful and repulsive Roman city. So when, in that place, Peter declares Jesus to be the Christ, Jesus is understandably alarmed. Jesus knows what "messiah" means in the minds of those around him. He can see the anger and violence in their eyes. He knows their understanding falls short. He knows the image that they clutch is headed in the wrong direction.

And so, like the master that he is, Jesus rises. He rises as he did in the boat, to command the wind and the waves. But this time Jesus turns to Peter and to all of the disciples with him. With stern authority, he absolutely commands them to tell this falsehood to no one.

For all who read his Gospel, Mark has staged the scene beautifully. He lets us feel the impact of Jesus' command. Perhaps Mark believes that we too may sometimes misunderstand what it means to walk in the way of the Messiah. And perhaps Mark knows that those falsehoods that come close to the truth are often the most dangerous falsehoods of all.

Mark wants all of us who read his Gospel to be careful. If the seed is to grow in our hearts, and if we are to take up our bed and walk, then we must see with clarity, lest we fail to walk in God's true way.

For Discussion: If Jesus were with us today, what kinds of ideas about himself or about God might he order us, or other Christians, to tell to no one? How can we know which of our understandings are valid—and which go off in dangerously misguided directions?

TEXT TO READ: MARK 8:31-32A

FIRST COMMENT ON THE TEXT: After ordering the disciples not to tell anyone that he is the Messiah, Jesus begins telling them what will happen to him. It's very different from what people of Jesus' day might have expected of a messiah.

He begins by referring to himself as the Son of Man. He refuses to use any exalted title for himself. He doesn't call himself "messiah." He talks about himself as the Son of Man, which emphasizes his common characteristics with the disciples and with all of us who read Mark's Gospel. "Son of Man" literally means "offspring of Adam."

Then Jesus explains that he, as an ordinary human, will experience great suffering—the opposite of what people might expect in a triumphant, military-oriented messiah. In addition, he says, he will be rejected by the most powerful people in Jerusalem: the elders, the chief priests, and the scribes. Peter and others like him may expect a triumphant messiah who will rule as king in Jerusalem, with all of the powerful Jerusalem elite standing loyally at his side.

As they listen to Jesus' words, Peter and the disciples are amazed. If Jesus is a messiah, then he's not the kind of messiah they have in mind.

Then Jesus shocks them further. He tells them he will be killed. Not that he'll die of old age. Not that he'll die of some disease. Not that he'll fall in battle. But that he'll be killed. Executed. Slaughtered.

And just as the disciples are wondering what kind of awful new "way" this is, Jesus shocks them again. He declares that his execution at the hands of the state won't be the end. After three days, he says, he'll rise again. Like the paralyzed man whom he told to take up his bed and walk, Jesus will take up his grave and rise. Death won't hold him in the ground. And execution at the hands of the state won't put an end to anything he's begun.

For Discussion: What do you think the disciples are thinking or feeling as they hear Jesus' words? Why do you think Mark makes such a point of saying that Jesus speaks these things openly? What sort of spin do you think Mark is putting on these comments by saying that?

SECOND COMMENT ON THE TEXT: Mark presents Jesus as one who walks a new path. He leads his disciples down a new way. It is a way they don't understand very well. So Jesus warns them that suffering, rejection, and even death lie ahead. But none of that will deter Jesus. None of that will hold Jesus back. For even after the ultimate punishment, he will rise again. Even after a mighty army puts him to death, he will still be marching on.

In a gospel song, Dallas Holm perfectly expresses Jesus' sentiments:

> *Go ahead, drive the nails in my hands.*
> *Laugh at me where I stand;*
> *Go ahead and say it isn't me—*
> *the day will come when you will see!*
> *'Cause I'll rise again.*
> *There's no power on earth can tie me down!*
> *Yes, I'll rise again—death can't keep me in the ground![1]*

Mark wants those of us who walk in Jesus' way to know that powerful forces may try to intimidate us. We may be threatened with suffering, rejection, or death. But none of that needs to hold us back. We can take up the threats and follow. We can pick up our beds and walk. For there's a rising just ahead.

And by walking with Jesus in God's new way, we'll be walking in the way of love, in the way of nonviolence, in the way that Dr. Martin Luther King Jr. said was the only way that would ever lead to reconciliation, redemption, and "the creation of a beloved community." For Mark, this is the only path worth walking.

NOTE

1. "I'll Rise Again" by Dallas Holm. Reprinted by permission of the author.

... HE SAID UNTO THEM, WHOSOEVER WILL COME AFTER ME, LET HIM DENY HIMSELF, AND TAKE UP HIS CROSS, AND FOLLOW ME.
—MARK 8:34

WHERE THE BURDENS OF MY HEART ROLL AWAY

MARK 8:31-37

SETTING THE STAGE

Jesus and the disciples have gone to the region around Caesarea Philippi, a center of oppressive Roman power that is filled with temples built to honor the Roman caesar and the proud but petty rulers that the caesar has set over the impoverished people of Palestine.

In the midst of this symbol of all that the Jewish people want to throw off, Jesus asks his disciples who they think he is. Peter immediately calls Jesus "the messiah," which is understood in that day as a political savior who will raise an army and march into Jerusalem, slaughtering all those who have oppressed the Jewish people. The geographic area in which they are traveling undoubtedly influences Peter's answer. His hopes have been aroused. His political passions are chomping at the bit.

But this political understanding of what it means to be messiah is exactly what Jesus is trying to repudiate. So with great force, he commands Peter and the other disciples to tell no one such a falsehood. That's not it at all, says Jesus—and don't you dare tell anyone otherwise!

TEXT TO READ: MARK 8:31-32A

For Discussion: What do these verses tell us about the relationship of Jesus to the political and religious authorities of his day? In what ways might Jesus have scandalized the political and religious powers of our day?

COMMENT ON THE TEXT: Mark is ready to lead us headlong down a path to deeper understanding. So immediately he shows us Jesus speaking with the disciples about the suffering and rejection he will face from the Jerusalem establishment. This is the opposite of what they might have expected in a political messiah.

Jesus further tells the disciples that he will be "killed." His death will be violent, he tells them, and it will come at the hands of the state. We aren't told the disciples' reaction. But we can presume their horror. Then, just as quickly, Jesus assures the disciples that three days after he is killed, he will "rise again." This too is an astounding claim.

According to the Hebrew Scriptures, two people from the olden days were so close to God that when the time came to die, they rose to be with God. One was Enoch. The other was Elijah. But according to historical documents, some Jews also believed that the same thing happened to Moses. Deuteronomy describes Moses' death and even says that Moses was buried. But apparently some devout Jews of Jesus' day believed that Moses too had risen to be with God. They pointed to the times that he climbed Mount Sinai to hear the words of God and the glory that seemed to transform his face. They believed that instead of dying, anyone who was as close to God as Moses was would surely be raised to be with God.

How did they justify their belief despite the biblical record? Their interpretation was that the words of Deuteronomy describing Moses' death were written in anticipation, by Moses himself, prior to Moses' death. They felt it was only natural that Moses, given his humility, would not describe himself as rising to be with God, even though that's what they thought had surely happened.

So when Jesus says that after three days he'll rise again, he's not only making an advance comment about his resurrection. He's also putting himself in the company of people like Enoch and Elijah and Moses—people that many Jews felt had been especially close to God.

TEXT TO READ: MARK 8:32B

For Discussion: Why do you think Peter rebuked Jesus? What was there about what Jesus said that provokes this response from Peter? Sometimes we think that we're better than Peter. But are there things that Jesus might say to us, if he were here, that might provoke us to rebuke him too? What parts of Jesus' message do we find it hardest to accept?

TEXT TO READ: MARK 8:33

FIRST COMMENT ON THE TEXT: Peter has taken Jesus aside. Perhaps he's put his arm around his back and called him off the path into a quiet place, away from the other disciples. Peter is upset at something Jesus has said. And instead of being Jesus' disciple, Peter now tries to be Jesus' teacher. Mark says that Peter rebukes Jesus. Peter tries to set Jesus straight. He angrily challenges what Jesus has said. Peter's one concession is that he takes Jesus aside before issuing his rebuke. Apparently Peter doesn't want to embarrass Jesus in front of the other disciples.

But Jesus won't be detached from the others. Mark tells us that he catches the eyes of the other disciples—just as he wants to catch our eyes when one of us goes wrong. And then, keeping the disciples in view, Jesus rebukes Peter.

Mark's description of this scene is dramatic. "Peter," of course, is a nickname. It means "stone" or "rock." Peter's real name is Simon. And now Jesus is about to call Simon another name as well. Mark tells us that Jesus turns on the one he calls Stone, the one whose name means Rocky Ground. And Jesus says, "Get thee behind me, Satan!"

By telling Peter to get behind him, Jesus is telling Peter to return to the role of disciple. In these days, when disciples travel with their teacher, the teacher walks in front and the disciple walks behind. In a way, Jesus is telling Peter to get back where he belongs—for he has much yet to learn.

SECOND COMMENT ON THE TEXT: The name *Satan* may seem harsh. But the reason for this vigorous response can be seen in the words that Mark includes. Jesus calls Peter "Satan" because he savors not divine things but human things. In other words, his mind is fixed on human ways instead of God's ways. In the eyes of Mark, Jesus has made it clear. Human ways are Satan's ways. And we who follow Jesus—we who wish to walk behind him in the way of the Lord—must learn to see the world from God's eyes. We need to see possibilities where humans would tell us that all hope is lost. And we need to choose means of attaining those possibilities that are in keeping with God's character.

Mark doesn't tell us what it is that causes Peter to rebuke Jesus. Mark focuses instead on Jesus' response. For it's in the response of Jesus to Peter that we can be challenged. Mark is saying that even we who call ourselves disciples can focus on the old ways of this world rather than on the new ways of God. We can close ourselves off from divine possibilities. We can deny the transforming power of peace and grace and love. We can choose instead the old ways of violence and exclusion and hate. But when we do so, says Mark, we better get our ears ready. For somewhere in the distance, there will be the voice of Jesus saying, "Get behind me, Satan! Can't you see what God is up to? Can't you set your heart—and hands—on the ways of God?"

For Discussion: What are some of the ways of God that Christians today find it hardest to follow in? What would it take to get more Christians to break free from the limited ways of thinking that Satan traps us in? How can we begin to savor the ways of God?

TEXT TO READ: MARK 8:34

FIRST COMMENT ON THE TEXT: In Mark's drama, Jesus has rebuked Peter for savoring the ways of this world rather than the ways of God. The rebuke is to Peter, but throughout the rebuke, Jesus keeps his eyes on the disciples as well. Now Mark expands the scene even further. Jesus calls in the crowd as well as the disciples. A great multitude mills about on the stage of Mark's drama, ready for whatever Jesus has to say. And we can only guess that Mark wants us to see ourselves on that stage as well, there in the crowd, listening to Jesus.

For Discussion: According to Mark 8:34, what are the three essential steps that Jesus lists for all those who seek to be in his company? Scholars have debated these words for centuries and often come to very different conclusions. But what do you think they mean? What is Mark trying to tell us?

SECOND COMMENT ON THE TEXT: The first thing Jesus says is to "deny" yourself. Some people think that when Jesus says "deny" yourself, he means deny your personal desires. Don't allow yourself any pleasures. Ignore your emotions. Live in as much agony as possible. Eat only the bare minimum needed for survival. And never, ever let a smile cross your face.

But it's possible that Jesus means something else, something connected to this context in Mark. Jesus has just rebuked Peter for focusing on the ways of this world rather than on the ways of God. Jesus has called Peter "Satan." And perhaps it is the Satan in each of us that we must deny. Perhaps Jesus is saying, "Set aside the old ways of thinking. Quit savoring the things of Satan—the violence, the hate, the fear, the greed, the grudges, the seeking of glory or wealth for ourselves at the expense of others, the spirit of retaliation, the failure to love and uphold our neighbor, the failure to forgive." Perhaps Jesus is telling us to stop thinking in these old ways, these ways that hold us back and hold us down, these ways that hurt and harm, these ways that leave the world in such misery.

Perhaps Mark is telling us that when Satan gets into you and when the spirit of Satan takes over your mind, as it did for Peter, then you have to deny that part of yourself which has become Satan. And if so, then the first step in discipleship is to cast off all that we have within ourselves that is not grounded in the beautiful and holy ways of God.

THIRD COMMENT ON THE TEXT: The next thing Jesus says is to "take up [your] cross." Some people think that when Jesus says "take up your cross," he means that we should expect to stagger through life under an incredible load of worries and troubles of all kinds. And they think that when worries and troubles come, we should neither complain nor seek relief.

Others think that Jesus isn't referring to the worries of life but political persecution. They argue that in Jesus' day, the cross is used for only one thing: political control. It's the people who get out of hand that Roman rulers hang on crosses. These troublemakers are hung naked on crosses in public places to suffer a slow, humiliating death. It's a form of public torture. Its purpose is to intimidate and control anyone else who might speak up or otherwise act against the power of Rome. The cross is used for anyone who opposes injustice. It's used against rabble-rousers and revolutionaries. It's used against terrorists and freedom fighters, most of whom survive by stealing from the rich and thus are branded as thieves.

The cross was certainly a form of social control. But some of the people who recognize its political dimensions miss the boat in another way. They think that what Jesus is saying is that if we are truly disciples, we need to be burdened by persecution, imprisonment, and death. They almost feel like there's something wrong if they aren't being persecuted or incapacitated in some way by the powers of our day. Maybe they have a martyr complex. Or maybe not. But it's almost as if they think Jesus has told his followers to encourage their own persecution.

However, if we are to properly understand what Jesus is thinking, we have to look both at the cross and at what we are to do with the cross, which is to take it up. In Mark's Gospel, Jesus doesn't tell his followers to nail themselves to a cross. Nor does he tell his followers to bear the cross. Or be weighed down by the cross. Rather, he tells them to take it up.

FOURTH COMMENT ON THE TEXT: The meaning of the Greek word that Mark uses for "take up" does not imply being weighed down by something. It means the opposite. For example, this same Greek word is used in Acts 27:13 to mean to "loose anchor," to take up the weight that is holding you down, so that you can sail on. Likewise, this same Greek word is used in Mark 2:9, where Jesus commands a paralyzed man to take up his bed and walk. Later in Mark, this same Greek word is used to describe how faith gives us the power to pick up a mountain that's in our way and cast it aside.

By including this scene in his Gospel, Mark wants us to know that political powers may indeed seek to intimidate us and control us. More often than not, they will be stuck in the mindset of Satan. They will do things that we must deny. But we aren't to let their threats of a cross control us. We aren't to let their power get us down.

Mark is reminding us that the principalities and powers will try to use the cross and its modern equivalents as a means of enslavement and control. But if the world throws us a cross, we aren't supposed to accept it. We should take it up. We should yank it out of the ground and move on. The cross isn't to be the place where the world gains control over us. In the words of an old hymn, the cross is to be that place "where the burdens of our heart roll away."

In his words to the crowd, Jesus reminds us that if we are to follow in God's new way, we can't let crosses slow us down—and we can't let any oppressor hold us back. We have to take up our bed and walk. We have to take up our cross and follow. We have to take up the mountains that rise in our path and run on in God's new way. It is a message about liberation, not enslavement. Jesus is reminding us about breaking free.

For Discussion: What are the modern equivalents of the cross as a means of social and political control? What does throwing off the cross mean in our day? What weights and burdens do we need to roll away?

FIFTH COMMENT ON THE TEXT: The last thing that Jesus says is to "follow me." Some people think that they follow Jesus by announcing that they've decided to become a Christian. They forget that Jesus never calls himself "Christian." The word isn't even known in Jesus' day. He is a practicing Jew. And as for labels, all that he calls himself is "Son of Man," which is a way of identifying himself with all of humanity, not just a member of a specific religious group.

Others think that they follow Jesus by being active in a church. They forget that Jesus never sets foot in a church. He attends Jewish synagogues and temples. But his most intimate spiritual conversations are in homes or beside the road—or wherever people are in need.

When Jesus says "follow me," he isn't thinking of a label and he isn't thinking of our joining some new organization. He is thinking of the way that God is making through the wilderness. He is calling each of us to walk in the new ways of God. He is calling each of us to live in love and peace and grace. He is calling each of us to forgive and embrace and transform. He is calling each of us to join him in truly savoring the things of God. He is calling on each of us to make God's ways our own.

TEXT TO READ: MARK 8:35-37

For Discussion: Through his words and questions, do you think Jesus is urging his followers to lose their lives or save their lives? What is the overall point he is trying to make?

COMMENT ON THE TEXT: These statements and questions from Jesus are filled with irony and paradox. Because they raise such fundamental issues, people sometimes take them out of context and quote them as if

Jesus raised them out of the blue, as if they were meant to stand alone. But in Mark's Gospel they are very much a part of the larger context. And that larger context helps us understand their meaning.

Jesus has just told his followers to take up their crosses and follow him. He has indicated that there will be many efforts to control us. Governing rulers will issue threats, even threats of death. Powerful forces will seek to shackle us. Heavy burdens will be piled on our shoulders. Mountains will rise in our path. The mindset of Satan will infiltrate our hearts.

But Jesus says that when we walk with faith and not with fear, these threats and shackles and mountains can be taken up and set aside. We don't have to be intimidated. We don't have to be threatened. We don't have to be kept from walking in the new way that God is making through the wilderness. We can take up our beds and walk.

Threats gain their power by making us think that if we rock the boat, we'll lose our life. Burdens nail us to the ground by making us believe that anything else will be too dangerous. As a result, the strongest shackles are often the shackles in our minds. We're afraid to break loose. We're afraid to break free. We're afraid to lose the only life we know for the sake of that which we must accept in faith.

When Jesus tells his followers that anyone who wants to "save his [or her] life will lose it," he's telling us that we can let threats and shackles and political intimidation govern our hearts. But by giving in to fears and threats, we won't save our lives. We will lose them.

What Jesus wants his followers to do is to let loose of those fears and burdens that we grasp so tightly. For when we let loose of the fears that control us, we're free to walk with Jesus. We're free to believe the gospel—the good news that God is close at hand, that the big bully has been bound, that our helper is the Mighty One in whom all power flows.

BACKGROUND TEXT TO READ: EXODUS 1:8-9,15-17

For Discussion: In what ways do the actions of Shiphrah and Puah illustrate or not illustrate the kind of actions that Jesus is calling us to?

COMMENT ON THE TEXT: An old spiritual expresses the same thought with these words:

> *Father, I stretch my hands to thee, no other help I know.*
> *If thou withdraw thyself from me, oh, whither shall I go?*

Perhaps Jesus is saying that to stretch our hands to God, we must let loose of those things that we're clutching. We have to give up our fears. We have to set aside the threats. Even when friends leave us behind, we have to say, "Move, mountain! Mountain, get out of my way!"

Instead of grasping our shackles, we have to stretch our hands to God, the only help we know. For it's in stretching our hands to God that the world falls away. And in stretching our hands to God, we let loose of those things that the world, in seeking to control us, has made us think are so important.

Both in these verses and elsewhere, Mark's portrait of Jesus is a portrait of one who seeks to instill faith in the hearts of his disciples. Faith the size of a mustard seed. Faith to let go. Faith to cast down those things that oppress us. Faith to uproot those crosses onto which the world tries to nail us. Faith to let the burdens of our hearts be rolled away. And, most of all, the faith to follow Jesus—for the sake of the gospel, for the sake of love and hope and healing, for the sake of truly finding the grace that the world would like to deny.

In some hymnals, the old spiritual, "Father, I Stretch My Hands to Thee," has another verse, not as well known. But its words also speak to the point that Jesus is making:

> *Author of faith, to thee I lift, my weary, longing eyes.*
> *O let me now receive that gift—my soul without it dies!*

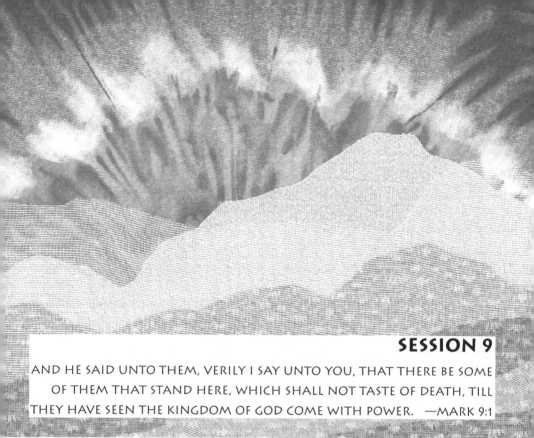

AND HE SAID UNTO THEM, VERILY I SAY UNTO YOU, THAT THERE BE SOME OF THEM THAT STAND HERE, WHICH SHALL NOT TASTE OF DEATH, TILL THEY HAVE SEEN THE KINGDOM OF GOD COME WITH POWER. —MARK 9:1

ROCKIN' JERUSALEM, RINGIN' THEM BELLS

MARK 8:38-9:13

Group leaders: This session, because of the nature of the biblical scene that is involved, is longer than most. If you are using this material as a group Bible study and if your time is strictly limited, you may need to break this session in half, even though you will thereby lose some continuity. If you must, stop just before reading Mark 9:8.

SETTING THE STAGE

We're in the dramatic midsection of Mark's Gospel. After forbidding his disciples from spreading any false rumors that he is a political savior, Jesus turns to the crowd. He says that all who want to walk in his way must deny themselves, take up their cross, and follow him.

In other words, they must deny Satan's efforts to control them. They must not be hindered by threats or intimidation. Rather, they must pull up any crosses that are thrown in their path. And then they must follow him. With faith and courage, they must live in God's new way—a way of love, a way of grace, a way of forgiveness, a way of nonviolence, a way that reaches out to all who are in need.

Finally, Jesus tells the crowd that by clutching to the life that the world has to offer, they are losing the life that God has to offer. Don't sell your soul, Jesus warns, for all true gifts come from above.

TEXT TO READ: MARK 8:38

For Discussion: Given the context, what do you think it means to be "ashamed" of Jesus and his words? What are the ways that we too might sometimes be ashamed of Jesus?

FIRST COMMENT ON THE TEXT: There are two time frames in this verse. First, Jesus speaks about the present. He speaks about those who, right then, are ashamed of him and his words. But then, in the second half of the verse, we see Jesus speaking of the future. Those who are ashamed of me now, he says, are the very ones that I will be ashamed of in the future.

Who are these people who are ashamed of Jesus and his words? Are they the ones who clutch their burdens? Are they the ones who believe the lies of this world? Are they the ones who think shackles are freedom? Are they the ones who are so filled with fear that faith can't find any room in their souls?

Well, says Jesus, one day they will be ashamed not of me and my message. Rather, they will be ashamed of themselves. For one day, says Jesus, they will stand in shame before God and the holy angels. One day, says Jesus, they will see the glory of which I speak—and will tremble in shame at their unbelief.

Notice also that Jesus describes those who are ashamed of him as being part of an "adulterous and sinful generation." These are people who have made love with the wrong god. They have believed the sinful lies of a dying power. And they have polluted their hearts with fears and burdens. In such a heart, the seed of faith finds no fertile ground.

SECOND COMMENT ON THE TEXT: In presenting these words from Jesus, Mark may be hoping that his readers will recall the words of those

Jewish prophets who addressed similar themes. For in the words of the prophets, we gain an even deeper sense of what Mark is telling us.

One such passage is found in Jeremiah 13:25-27, where it says,

> *This is your lot, the portion I have measured out to you, says the* LORD, *because you have forgotten me and trusted in lies. I myself will lift up your skirts over your face, and your shame will be seen. I have seen your abominations, your adulteries and neighings, your shameless prostitutions on the hills of the countryside. Woe to you, O Jerusalem! How long will it be before you are made clean?* (NRSV).

Jeremiah asks, How long will it be before God's people are made clean? How long will it be before they see their shame? How long will it be before they quit trusting in lies? How long will it be before they see that they're losing their soul?

THIRD COMMENT ON THE TEXT: Here in Mark, Jesus seems to answer Jeremiah's question. The Son of Man is coming, says Jesus. And he is coming "in the glory of his Father" and "with the holy angels."

This is quite an announcement, for it's the first time in the Gospel that Jesus refers to God as his Father. This must have been startling to the disciples, and Mark may expect us to be startled as well. Then Jesus makes the scene even more vivid by referring to the holy angels. It's as if Jesus is painting a picture for us. It's a picture of a grand celebration by the heavenly hosts—a great homecoming, as it were, a time when the glory of God is full and undisguised.

Deep within him, Jesus knows the time is coming. A new day is dawning. God's cleansing is close at hand. And already, to quote the words of an old spiritual, he can "hear the archangels, rockin' Jerusalem, ringin' them bells." Perhaps we too need bells ringing in our ears. Perhaps we too need to sense angels walking at our side. Perhaps we too need to let faith open our eyes. Perhaps we too need to lay down our burdens and stretch our hands to God. For then no cross can hold us down. No threat can hold us back. No lie can shackle our souls. Like Jesus, we'll be ready to walk with joy—"up the King's highway."

TEXT TO READ: MARK 9:1

For Discussion: What do you think Jesus means by the kingdom of God coming with power? What does it mean to see the kingdom's power?

COMMENT ON THE TEXT: "Taste death"? "Come in power"? This verse can be a bit confusing to modern readers. But it was likely much more clear to the people of Mark's day.

One thing that they would immediately understand is the reference to people who will "not taste death." According to some scholars, this phrase often had a specific meaning in the Jewish literature of Mark's day. It was used to describe people who never died. To Jews, this included Enoch, a person from Genesis who walked with God into heaven, plus Elijah, who is described in 2 Kings as riding to heaven in a chariot. It also included Moses, who was assumed to have been taken directly to heaven. These were special people, very close to God.

The second thing that we sometimes misunderstand about this verse is the use of the word *until*. Jesus says that there are some standing here who will not taste death until "they have seen the kingdom of God come with power." What we don't realize is that this is a common Hebrew way of speaking. Jews would often take two truths and link them with the word *until*. It didn't mean that one wouldn't happen until the other had happened. It simply meant that both would happen. It was a way of expressing certainty and assurance.

So in effect Jesus is saying that some of those special people who never died are going to see the kingdom of God coming to earth with power. In his preaching, Jesus said that the kingdom of God is close at hand. Now he's saying that some of God's special people, people who never died, are going to see that reality for themselves.

In Mark's fast-moving drama, the very scene that Jesus refers to is about to unfold. It will be fantastic. It will be mind-blowing. And it will be dramatically revealing, for some of those who never died will soon see the kingdom of God moving forward with power . . .

TEXT TO READ: MARK 9:2-3

For Discussion: When does Mark say this next event happens? Do you think he does or doesn't see the timing as significant? Where does Mark say Jesus goes? Most people describe the geography of Galilee as hilly, rather than mountainous. So why do you think Mark might have described the place as he does? Who does Jesus take with him? Why do you think these three are chosen? How are Jesus' clothes described? Do you notice anything significant about this description?

COMMENT ON THE TEXT: The scene here is dramatic. Jesus goes up a "high mountain" with three of his first disciples, Peter, James, and John. When they get up the mountain, Jesus' appearance begins to change. The text says he is "transfigured." His clothing becomes dazzling white. Mark says his clothes become whiter than anyone "on earth" could ever bleach them. The obvious implication is that they're been transformed by Someone who is not on earth. Mark wants us to know that we're going beyond the realm of the human.

TEXT TO READ: MARK 9:4

For Discussion: What significance do you think Mark sees in the fact that Elijah and Moses appear on the mountain, talking with Jesus? As this scene unfolds, how do you think the three disciples are feeling?

COMMENT ON THE TEXT: Mark fashions this scene so that we see it through the eyes of the disciples. And what a scene! Elijah and Moses are ancient leaders of the Jewish faith. They occupy places of honor in an esteemed religious tradition. In the Jewish world, Elijah and Moses are understood to have been so close to God that they never tasted death. It's believed that when death approached, God drew them to heaven.

These two are among God's most special servants. And here they are, talking with Jesus, as if they and Jesus are partners. As if they and Jesus already know each other. As if they and Jesus are somehow working for the same Ruler. As if they and Jesus are part of a cosmic struggle running through the ages. We can almost feel the disciples' mouths dropping open. We can almost hear the heavy pounding of their hearts. We can almost see their eyes bugging out. They are experiencing something that goes beyond themselves.

TEXT TO READ: MARK 9:5-6

COMMENT ON THE TEXT: Peter has blundered twice before in this part of Mark. He confesses to the wrong understanding of Jesus, and Jesus firmly orders him to tell his views to no one. Then Peter boldly takes Jesus aside and tries to rebuke him. In response, Jesus calls him "Satan" and orders him to get back where he belongs.

Now here is Peter, once again, shooting off his mouth. He barges into the conversation among Elijah, Moses, and Jesus, suggesting that the disciples build three "tabernacles" or dwellings on the mountain, one for Elijah, one for Moses, one for Jesus. These would be places of honor and worship, a holy shrine to each of them.

It is a stupid thing to say. But Mark explains that Peter and the disciples are terrified. They are "sore afraid." So they don't know what to say. Silence would have been better. But apparently Peter is not the silent type. And once again, he's put his foot in his mouth. He's misunderstood entirely. He's lost sight of the way of the LORD. What Jesus is calling him to is not the construction of holy shrines but active involvement in the ongoing journey of faith.

Mark gives us a clue, right off the bat, that Peter is once again talking crazy. The clue comes in the first word he speaks. "Rabbi," he says. Or "Master." This is the kind of formal, honorary title that Jesus has never sought for himself. In the Gospel of Mark, the word *rabbi* is used for Jesus only three times. Once is here, when Peter in fear says the wrong thing. The same word is used later when Peter disputes with Jesus about the temple. And the final time is when Judas betrays Jesus with a kiss, addressing him, in that fatal moment, as "rabbi." For the Gospel of Mark, "rabbi" is not a positive word.

TEXT TO READ: MARK 9:7-8

For Discussion: If the disciples are already terrified, how do you think they feel when a cloud surrounds them and then from the cloud comes a voice? What is it that the voice declares? What is it that the voice commands?

FIRST COMMENT ON THE TEXT: In Mark's drama, Jesus never responds to Peter's suggestion that the disciples build three shrines on the mountain. Nor does Jesus respond to Peter's use of the word *rabbi*. Mark simply gives us a voice from on high. It comes from the cloud. It doesn't say, "This is your messiah." It doesn't say, "This is your rabbi." Rather, the voice says, "This is my Son. This is my beloved."

According to the voice in the cloud, Jesus' identity comes from his relationship to God. Jesus, the disciples are told, is a child of the Most High. He is the offspring of the Divine. He walks in God's way, as any loyal child does. So he is beloved. So he is treasured.

In Jewish thought, God is sometimes seen as a kind of divine king.

Similarly, the son of a king is thought of as sharing in the qualities and character of the king. Peter, James, and John have gone up the mountain with Jesus, who has continually told others that the kingdom of God is close at hand, that the power of God is not far off, and that the reign of God is ready to take root in our hearts.

Now, in the midst of a swirling cloud, in the presence of Elijah and Moses, the disciples hear the voice of God, the voice of the heavenly King. The voice says Jesus is the King's Son. So in effect, he too is a king. He too is part of God's cosmic plan. He too is playing a role in the ongoing battle of good against evil, love against hate, grace against judgment, peace against violence, generosity against greed.

Then the voice addresses the three disciples directly. "Hear him," the voice says. "Listen."

In Mark 4 we find Jesus' story about a sower going out to sow seed. And in explaining the parable, Jesus says that the seed is the word of God. And now the voice from the cloud tells us, in effect, that the word is Jesus. Mark is reminding us that no matter what is happening in our world and no matter the problems in our own lives, it is Jesus we must hear. In the voice of Jesus, the seed is planted.

After presenting the story about the sower, Mark quotes Jesus as saying, "Let anyone with ears to hear listen!" (Mark 4:23, NRSV). Mark also suggests that to those that hear, more will be given (Mark 4:24-25). If we are to have the strength to take up our crosses and follow, if we are to have the faith to take up our beds and walk, if we are to be breaking free, then we need to hear. We need to listen. We need to let the words of Jesus take root in our hearts.

For Discussion: In addressing Peter, James, and John, the voice from the cloud doesn't say, "Thanks for hearing him." It doesn't say, "You fellas have sure listened well." It says, "Hear him." What does that suggest about how well the disciples are doing? Why do you think it was so hard for them? Why is it so hard for us to hear Jesus?

SECOND COMMENT ON THE TEXT: Many of us aren't as familiar with the Jewish Scriptures as people were in Jesus' day. As a result, we often miss some of the deep meaning that early believers would have seen in the things that Jesus says and does. So sometimes we have to force ourselves to go back and look at those old texts. In the Jewish Scriptures, we find texts that shed new light on what we're reading.

The story of Jesus' transfiguration, with a voice coming from the cloud, is no exception. It contains echoes of two prominent stories from the Jewish Scriptures, one in Daniel, one in Exodus. And those stories give us a deeper sense of what this is all about.

For example, Daniel 10 (NRSV) describes a time of violent political turmoil, a time of "great conflict" (v. 1). Daniel is distressed. He has "been mourning for three weeks" (v. 2). He falls into a trance. He sees a figure, "clothed in linen, with a belt of gold" (v. 5). The figure's face is "like lightning," and the figure's arms and legs have "the gleam of burnished bronze" (v. 6).

"My strength left me," Daniel says (Daniel 10:8, NRSV). In fear, he falls to the ground. "But then a hand touched me," he remembers, "and roused me to my hands and knees" (v. 10). The voice then says, "Daniel, greatly beloved, pay attention to the words that I am going to speak to you" (v. 11). The voice expresses great awareness of the troubles of the world, the political turmoil, the violent struggles (v. 13). Daniel describes his pain, his fears, his sense of exhaustion. "I am shaking," Daniel says. "No strength remains in me, and no breath is left in me" (v. 17). Then the one who shines like lightning touches Daniel again and strengthens him, saying, "Do not fear, greatly beloved. You are safe. Be strong and courageous!" (v.18).

THIRD COMMENT ON THE TEXT: In like manner, Exodus 24 describes Moses going up a mountain to meet God, and at one point he seems to take with him Aaron, Nadab, and Abihu, three of his associates (v. 9). According to the text, "the glory of the LORD settled on Mount Sinai, and the cloud covered it for six days" (v. 16, NRSV). After six days, the same time period mentioned in Mark 9:2, the Lord calls to Moses out of the cloud (v. 16).

The Lord then gives Moses instructions that he is to pass on to the people of Israel. He is entrusted with what God wants the people to hear. But Moses comes down from the mountain and finds that the people have lost faith. They've built a golden calf—and begun to worship it. In horror, Moses smashes the stone tablets he's been given.

As a result, Moses must go up the mountain again. And this time, he is visibly transfigured (Exodus 34:29). According to the text, "the skin of his face shone because he had been talking with God" (v. 29, NRSV). When Moses returns to the people, he begins to address the people, saying, "These are the things that the LORD has commanded you to do" (Exodus 35:1, NRSV).

For Discussion: What similarities do you see between the account in Daniel and in Mark? Between Exodus and Mark? What are the dominant themes of the Daniel story? Of the Exodus story? What do these tell us about Jesus' transfiguration?

Note: If you are breaking this session in half due to time constraints, this is the place to stop. When you resume, you can reestablish the context by first rereading Mark 9:2-7.

TEXT TO READ: MARK 9:8

For Discussion: How do you think the disciples feel when, all of a sudden, the scene changes?

COMMENT ON THE TEXT: The scene on the mountain is incredible. Somehow the disciples' eyes are opened. They see Jesus talking with Elijah and Moses, two people who served God in special ways, two people who never tasted death, two people who were taken directly into God's presence.

Then a voice comes from heaven, declaring that Jesus too has a special relationship with God. He is like a child of the Almighty. He is beloved. He is special. And they are to listen to him. They are to hear what he has to say. For he is God's word, a seed waiting to be planted, a seed waiting to take root.

The disciples have trembled in fear, stood in shock, and spoken in ignorance. They have been overcome with awe. Probably they have also felt confusion and panic and a deep sense of bewilderment. But then, just as suddenly, the cloud disappears. Elijah and Moses can't be found. The voice is silent. They look around. No one is there—but Jesus.

Is it a dream? Have they been in a trance? Has it been some kind of spiritual ecstasy? Did they fall asleep? Are they only imagining? Surely they wonder. Yet it seems so real. It seems so clear. We imagine them frantically spinning around, wondering if Elijah and Moses have stepped out of sight somewhere. We imagine them searching the sky, wondering where the cloud has gone. We imagine them hushing each other, desperately wanting to hear another word from the voice that seemed so close.

But the hillside is empty. The sky is clear. Silence reigns. Everywhere they turn, there is stillness. No one is there—but Jesus.

For Discussion: Do you think Mark wants us to see some significance in the ending of this story? Have any of you, or anyone you know, ever had a spiritual vision or other unusual experience that left you feeling that God had been unusually close? When this experience on the mountain came to an end, do you think the disciples felt like they understood Jesus better—or understood him less? Why?

TEXT TO READ: MARK 9:9-10

For Discussion: If you had been Peter, James, or John, and if you had just had an experience like they have, would you find it easy or hard to do as Jesus has asked? Why?

COMMENT ON THE TEXT: As Jesus and the disciples come down the mountain, we imagine Peter, James, and John turning over in their minds what they have seen. They relive every moment. They call forth every memory, to be sure there's nothing they've missed.

And each time they turn it over in their minds, the more amazing it gets. Perhaps they're imagining the faces of the other disciples when they tell them. Perhaps they're anticipating how best to explain what's happened. But then Jesus punctures their balloon. And baffles them again. He orders them to tell no one of what they have seen. We imagine their hearts sinking. After what they've seen, after what they've heard, they are to tell no one? How can this be?

Then comes the most baffling statement of all. Don't tell anyone, Jesus says, until after the Son of Man has risen from the dead.

The disciples have just heard a voice declare Jesus to be God's Son. They have heard a voice say that Jesus is God's beloved. And there, on the mountain, they have seen him talking with Elijah and Moses, two people who never tasted death. So why is he talking about being dead, they might wonder. Elijah and Moses simply rose. For Elijah and Moses, according to Jewish teaching, death never came.

With his great sense of drama, Mark shows us Jesus leading the way down the hillside. The disciples follow, whispering to themselves. They don't dare speak aloud. After all, Jesus has told them to say nothing to anyone about what they've seen. But they keep trying to figure out what Jesus means by talking about his "rising from the dead."

For Discussion: What do you think it is that puzzles Peter, James, or John about the rising from the dead?

TEXT TO READ: MARK 9:11

COMMENT ON THE TEXT: In Mark's Gospel, Jesus and the three disciples are still on their way down the mountain. Peter, James, and John have been wondering about the "rising from the dead." But now their minds move on to other topics.

Having just seen Jesus with Elijah and Moses, they're wondering about something they've heard the scribes say. The scribes are the religious scholars of Jesus' day. And apparently some of the scribes have talked about a future time when Elijah will return to Israel. Something about this puzzles the disciples. So they ask Jesus about it.

For Discussion: Do you notice anything unusual about the disciples' question? If Elijah is to come first, what is to come next?

BACKGROUND TEXT TO READ: MALACHI 4:1-3

For Discussion: What do you think a text like this would mean to people in Mark's day, when common people suffer under the hands of the proud and arrogant, when life is precarious, when evildoers steal from the poor, when violence is everywhere, and when the rich constantly make alliances with whichever power has the strongest army?

COMMENT ON THE TEXT: Jewish people in Jesus' day have a strong sense of history and of God's ongoing promise. In the midst of their suffering, they look for the coming day of the Lord, a time when the wicked will no longer thrive, a time when the proud will be brought low, a time when the young will frolic like a calf, a time when people will know that their future is secure. They know this day might not come right away. They know it might take generations, even centuries. But they know it is coming.

The people of Jesus' day are a lot like the slaves of a later day. They recognize their troubles. They acknowledge their misery. They don't deny their oppression. But although they feel "like a motherless child," they sing "glory hallelujah" anyhow. For they know a change is coming. They know the day of the Lord will dawn. They know, deep in their hearts, that "trouble don't last alway."

The prophet Malachi wrote in faith about the coming day of the Lord, a time when the world would be set right. As a result, many poor folk in Palestine, as well as their scribes and religious scholars, think the coming day of the Lord will be a day of triumph and celebration, a day that will dawn without hardship or setback. They think that Elijah will pave the way for the day of the Lord by reappearing to restore human hearts and mend broken relationships. Their belief is based on their interpretation of the last two verses of Malachi.

BACKGROUND TEXT TO READ: MALACHI 4:5-6

COMMENT ON THE TEXT: When Mark is written, the people of Palestine are enduring much wickedness. Violence is everywhere. A few people grab all the wealth, while the vast majority live in great poverty. There is terror and oppression. Sometimes people don't know where their next meal is coming from.

So it isn't surprising if they are longing for the "great and dreadful day of the LORD," a time when the wicked will be punished and evil wiped away. But according to Malachi, Elijah will have to come first and restore human hearts, restore human relationships, and draw the righteous back to God. And that might be a bit frustrating to some people, because it seems to postpone the promise of God.

When Mark shows us the three disciples asking Jesus about the teaching of the scribes who say that Elijah must come first, he is putting into the disciples' mouths a question that likely echoes in many people's hearts. In effect, the disciples are asking, will there be a long delay before we see the day of the Lord? Must we wait for Elijah before having any hope that God will come and wipe out this evil from our midst?

TEXT TO READ: MARK 9:12

COMMENT ON THE TEXT: In his answer, Jesus tries to move the disciples toward a deeper level of understanding. But for many of us, Jesus' answer is puzzling. Jesus seems to be going off in a different direction, almost as if he's addressing a different subject. And so we wonder what in the world Jesus is talking about.

The King James Version is particularly confusing here, but more modern translations can be unclear as well. One reason for our confusion is that, unlike the original readers of Mark, we don't understand the ways that Jews of Jesus' day would discuss apparent contradictions in Scripture. According to some Bible scholars, what Jesus is doing here is trying to help his disciples see and understand the relationship between different biblical themes. And by using Jesus' answer in this way, Mark hopes to move us to a deeper understanding of God's word in Scripture as well.

The disciples have asked Jesus a question about whether Elijah must come before the great day of the Lord. And instead of answering directly, Jesus responds with two questions, each of which reflects a different biblical theme.

Jesus' first question draws out the usual interpretation of Elijah's role. "So Elijah," says Jesus, "when he comes first, he restores all things?" If Jesus and the disciples were on stage in front of us, we would see the disciples nodding in agreement. "Yes, of course," they might say. "Elijah comes first, restores all things, and then, after that, comes the great day of the Lord, in which evil disappears and all the wicked are immediately destroyed."

Jesus then offers a second question. "Well, then," he asks, "how is it that the Son of Man will suffer many things and be rejected?" In other words, Jesus is saying, if Elijah is going to restore all things, and if Elijah is going to restore human hearts and human relationships, and if, soon after that, there is going to be a mighty day of the Lord in which goodness suddenly triumphs over badness and evil is no more, then why does Scripture talk about me as one who will suffer and be rejected and even be killed? If the triumph will be easy, why do Isaiah and Zechariah and Daniel and even some of the psalms talk about the setbacks and anguish that servants of God will endure?

By including this conversation between Jesus and the disciples, Mark is reminding his readers that the day of the Lord is not as simple and quick as some people imagine. He's reminding us that the way of the Lord comes with struggle, suffering, and pain. We who seek to walk in God's way may experience rejection. We may be rebuked and scorned. We may feel that the world is passing us by. But Mark wants us to know that the day is coming. Never should our courage waver. Trouble may endure for a time. But trouble won't last alway.

TEXT TO READ: MARK 9:13

FIRST COMMENT ON THE TEXT: When Jewish scholars used a series of questions to explore the relationship between different themes in Scripture, they often ended with a concluding statement. This concluding statement would bring together in one place the answer to each of the questions, and by bringing those answers together, the concluding statement would move the hearer to a deeper level of understanding.

So Mark ends this discussion with a concluding statement from Jesus.

While the disciples are still shaking their heads in confusion, while the disciples are still puzzling over how to bring together these different themes, Jesus offers the answer. "Verily, I say unto you," he says, "Elijah has come. And instead of being welcomed, he was destroyed. For they did to him 'whatsoever they listed.' He sought to restore humanity. He sought to do what God wanted. But instead of being restored, they did to him what they wanted."

Jesus is not talking about a literal Elijah. For Jesus, "Elijah" is John the Baptist. John preached repentance and sought to restore human hearts and human relationships. So he is the promised Elijah. But instead of listening, the powers did to him what they wanted.

SECOND COMMENT ON THE TEXT: The Greek word that is used here for "wanted" is the same Greek word that appears several times in the story of John's beheading (Mark 6:21-28). It seems as if Mark wants us to remember the wild party that Herod gave in celebration of his birthday. Rich lords and Roman officers gather together in a drunken orgy. Herod asks his stepdaughter to do an erotic dance, which delights the crowd immensely. To show his thanks, Herod then offers his stepdaughter whatever she wants. Before answering, she goes to her mother and asks, "What shall I want?" And her mother tells her to want the head of John the Baptist brought in on a platter.

Through Jesus' answer, Mark reminds us not to trust the desires of the high and mighty. They seek what they want, and what they want is power for themselves, glory for themselves, riches for themselves. The wants of the high and mighty may come down hard on those of us who walk in God's new way. For even Elijah, in the form of John the Baptist, has his head chopped off to satisfy the whims of a petty king.

Yes, Jesus says, the kingdom of God is close at hand. The day of the Lord is coming. But we must not expect it to be easy. Mountains and crosses will be thrown in our path. Storms and terrors will rise in the night. But through it all, we'll have a Mighty One at our side. Through it all, the day of the Lord will come ever closer. Through it all, we'll sing "glory, hallelujah," thanking God for "how we made it over."

For Discussion: Mark presents John the Baptist as a gift from God to the world, a part of God's unfolding plan that was undermined and destroyed by the wants of the rich and powerful. What are the gifts of God to our day that are being destroyed by the wants of evil hearts? In what ways do wants keep us from walking in God's new way? How can we help each other keep our courage strong, even through suffering and struggle?

THIRD COMMENT ON THE TEXT: This conversation between Jesus and the disciples concerning Elijah and the suffering Son of Man doesn't take place in a vacuum. Mark presents it as a conversation that occurs as Jesus and the disciples come down the Mount of Transfiguration.

When the Gospel of Mark is written, there isn't as rigid a distinction in many people's minds between the present and the future. And so it wouldn't be surprising if Mark understands the Transfiguration as having taken place in both the present and the future.

Mark presents it as something that happened in a certain place, at a certain time. But in a sense, it is also a vision into the future. It is as if the curtain has been drawn open. Peter, James, and John have been invited to look through the fog. They've been invited to look through the suffering and rejection that lies ahead. They've been invited to see beyond Jesus' cruel death at the hands of the state.

And there, in the future, they've seen a risen Jesus. They've seen Jesus, raised to be with God, raised to converse with Moses and Elijah. They've been reminded that even in the horrors that lie ahead, Jesus won't be forgotten. Jesus is beloved. Jesus will be raised. And God's kingdom will come with power. Trouble may endure for a night, but in the morning, there will be angels and archangels, "rockin' Jerusalem, ringin' them bells."

Sometimes, to keep going, to keep struggling, we need a vision of the future. We need a deep and abiding faith in where God is headed. Mark reminds his readers that the way won't be easy. But he also reminds us of where the way is going. And who walks before us. The point is not the suffering. The point is where the suffering leads.

FOURTH COMMENT ON THE TEXT: In March 1965, after marching for five days from Selma to Montgomery, Alabama, Dr. Martin Luther King Jr. stood before his followers in front of the Alabama state capitol and asked them to listen. He told them that the road ahead wouldn't be easy. There would be no broad highways or quick solutions. Much suffering still lay ahead.

But we won't be deterred, he declared. You can burn our churches. You can bomb our homes. You can beat our preachers and our young people. But it won't make a difference, he said with rising passion, for my people are on the move.

How long will it take us to get where we are going, he asked. Not long, he answered, for our eyes—they have seen the glory of the coming of the Lord. That's why our souls are swift to answer. That's why our feet, though oh so weary, still press on in joy. We have seen the future, he declared. We can feel it, deep inside—our God is marching on!

In like manner, Mark wants those who read his Gospel to be ready— ready for anything. The wants of the rich and powerful will still wring blood from the poor and the oppressed. Much suffering and discouragement may still lie in our path. But in the face of whatever comes, Mark wants us to sing, in the words of an old spiritual:

> *I ain't got weary yet, I ain't got weary yet,*
> *I been in the wilderness a mighty long time,*
> *and I ain't got weary yet!*
> *I been walking with the Savior, I been walking with the Lord,*
> *I been in the wilderness a mighty long time,*
> *and I ain't got weary yet!*

SESSION 10

AND STRAIGHTWAY
THE FATHER OF THE
CHILD CRIED OUT,
AND SAID WITH
TEARS, LORD, I
BELIEVE; HELP THOU
MINE UNBELIEF.
—MARK 9:24

LIKE A TREE PLANTED BY THE WATER

MARK 9:14-29

SETTING THE STAGE

The Gospel of Mark is a continuing story, and Mark links each new scene to those that have gone before. So to understand the whole of the Gospel, we have to keep looking back to those scenes through which we've come.

To best understand today's passage, one scene we need to remember is found in Mark 8:34-38, where Jesus tells the crowd that those who want to follow him must deny themselves. They must set aside the fears and worries that hold them down.

Crosses may be thrown down in our path. We may be threatened with political intimidation and death. The principalities and powers may try to nail us down and halt our progress. But Jesus urges us to pull up those crosses and follow him. Those in power may threaten us. But we're to take up our bed and walk. We're to take up our cross and follow. The threats are hollow. We won't lose our lives. We'll find them.

The next scene we ought to remember is found in Mark 9:1-13, where Jesus takes Peter, James, and John up a high mountain. On the mountain, the disciples see Elijah and Moses talking with Jesus, who has a dazzling glow. A cloud covers the mountain. The disciples tremble as a voice says, "This is my Son, my beloved. Listen to him!"

Then, in the scene we're about to examine, Mark shows us Jesus coming down the mountain. Back in Exodus, when Moses came down from Mount Sinai after talking with God, he wondered what the people were up to. And it wouldn't be surprising if Mark wants us to imagine Jesus wondering something similar. Peter, James, and John are with him, but what about the others? What are they doing? Have they remained strong? Is their faith sure?

TEXT TO READ: MARK 9:14

COMMENT ON THE TEXT: Coming down the mountain, Jesus finds his other disciples. There's "a great multitude" about them. Feelings are running high. We hear angry voices. In the scene as Mark portrays it, it's as if a group of high-strung scribes and religious scholars have come unglued. The King James Version describes the scribes as "questioning with them." Other versions say "arguing with them" or "disputing with them." In any case, Mark wants us to feel the tension. The place is in an uproar.

For Discussion: Mark doesn't say with whom the scribes are arguing. Who might it be? Mark has previously shown us the scribes criticizing Jesus, and we've seen Jesus responding masterfully. But now Mark shows us the scribes coming at the disciples while Jesus is away. How do you think these disciples feel? What kinds of situations give us similar feelings?

TEXT TO READ: MARK 9:15

For Discussion: What do you think Mark is suggesting by saying that when the people see Jesus, they are "greatly amazed"?

COMMENT ON THE TEXT: In describing the crowd's reaction to Jesus' return, Mark seems to be reminding us, once again, of Moses' journey up Mount Sinai. According to Exodus, when Moses came down after speaking with God a second time, his face shone. In older days, many people felt that something similar should be true of us as well. It might not be that our face literally begins to shine, but they felt that there ought to be something different about us after we've talked with God. As it says in an old spiritual:

> *I looked at my hands, and my hands were different.*
> *I looked at my feet, and my feet were different . . .*

BACKGROUND TEXT TO READ: EXODUS 34:29-31

For Discussion: What kind of point do you think Mark is trying to make by emphasizing the similarities between Moses and Jesus?

TEXT TO READ: MARK 9:16

COMMENT ON THE TEXT: The scene, as Mark describes it, is full of commotion. The religious authorities are lecturing the disciples, disputing with them about something. The disciples aren't used to this. A crowd has gathered. Suddenly Jesus appears. His appearance still glows from the transfiguration. The crowd is in awe.

Seeing the commotion, Jesus walks up to the scribes and demands to know what they're arguing with the disciples about. But the Greek words that Mark uses here also imply that Jesus is asking why. He wants to know not only what they are arguing about—but why. Why do they constantly try to halt the work of God? Why do they, as religious leaders, try to shake the resolve of those who are trying to move forward in the power and love of God?

For Discussion: Can you think of situations in our time in which certain religious authorities have questioned and disputed with those who were seeking to walk in the way of God? Can you think of situations in which certain misguided religious leaders have sought to stand in the way or otherwise tried to shake the confidence of those to whom God was speaking? Why do you think certain religious leaders, who ought to know better, are sometimes God's biggest stumbling blocks?

TEXT TO READ: MARK 9:17-18

COMMENT ON THE TEXT: Mark unfolds this scene with his usual sense of drama. Jesus asks the scribes what they're up to. He looks them in the eye and demands to know why they're once again trying to halt the progress of those whom God has called. But instead of giving us the scribes' answer, Mark opens our ears to the cry of one from the crowd.

From the multitude, a father steps forward. When he speaks, there is a tremble in his voice . . .

"I've brought my son," the man says. "He's the cause of all this trouble. And he's the one they're arguing about." As the man speaks, we can imagine Jesus nodding. We can imagine Jesus sighing. The situation is becoming all too clear.

The man has tears in his eyes. "At times," the man explains, "something takes hold of my son and causes him to be unable to speak. He has these terrible seizures. He falls to the ground. He foams at the mouth. He grinds his teeth. And his whole body becomes rigid. My heart aches for my son. My heart longs for him to be set free from this affliction. So I brought him to your disciples. I thought they could heal him. I thought they could free him. But they could not . . ."

For Discussion: At this point in the story, what kinds of feelings might be running through the heart of this father? What kinds of people today might be experiencing similar feelings as they approach God's people?

BACKGROUND TEXT TO READ: MARK 3:13-15

For Discussion: Twice in his Gospel, Mark tells us Jesus has given his disciples power to cast out demons. Yet in this new story, they "could not." Why do you think they were suddenly unable to do what Jesus had enabled them to do?

TEXT TO READ: MARK 9:19

(all except the last four words of the verse)

FIRST COMMENT ON THE TEXT: This verse gets to the heart of why Mark sees this story as so important. Jesus looks at those around him, calling them a "faithless generation." The scribes, who quarrel with his disciples—they have lost faith in the forgiving love of God. The disciples, whose confidence is undermined by the words of the scribes—their faith is too thin, their courage too weak. The crowd that wavers between hope and despair, the crowd that is so easily swayed—they too are a part of the faithless generation.

For Mark, the significance of this encounter is heightened by his memory of what happened the first time that Moses came down from Mount Sinai, as told in Exodus 32. Moses is gone a long time. The people give up hope that he will ever return. Seeing their faith slip away, Aaron and the priests build for the people a golden calf. So when Moses returns from the mountaintop, when Moses returns from speaking with God, he finds a faithless generation. A generation of people whose roots are too shallow, a generation whose faith and confidence in God has slipped away.

So now Mark shows us Jesus coming down from a high mountain, a place where he and Moses and Elijah have spoken with God. And Jesus too finds a faithless generation, a generation whose faith slips away when Jesus steps aside, a generation whose courage is too easily undermined. A generation tossed to and fro.

SECOND COMMENT ON THE TEXT: On the way down the mountain, Jesus has talked with Peter, James, and John about promises found in Malachi, promises that someone like Elijah will restore human hearts and renew human relationships, promises that the day of the Lord will come.

Malachi also contains reminders that religious leaders can stand in God's way. In Malachi 2:5 (NRSV), God describes "my covenant" as "a covenant of life and well-being." But then God turns to the priests who were to affirm and honor that covenant, and God says to them, "You have turned aside from the way; you have caused many to stumble by your instruction; you have corrupted the covenant" (Malachi 2:8, NRSV).

The accusations of Malachi against the priests and religious leaders get very specific. "You have shown partiality," God says (Malachi 2:9, NRSV). And you have forgotten that "one God created us" all (v. 10). Malachi goes on to call the religious leaders "faithless," for they have put limits on the all-inclusive love of God. And Malachi doesn't use the word *faithless* just once. He uses it five times (vv. 10,11,14,15,16) to address religious leaders who speak words of death rather than life, words of judgment rather than mercy, words of enslavement rather than freedom, words that disempower rather than enable.

THIRD COMMENT ON THE TEXT: It seems likely that Mark wants to remind us that we can be led astray by religious leaders and by all who forget that the covenant of God is "a covenant of life and well-being" (Malachi 2:5, NRSV). Thus all who seek to leave us in our misery, all who say that God's love is only for a few, and all who seek to shake the confidence of those who walk in God's new way—they are a faithless generation.

They have let faith slip through their fingers, and in blindness they seek to destroy the faith of others. They will batter us, Mark is saying. They will hassle us. They will seek to keep us from acting in God's own way. Sometimes they will shake our courage, maybe even slow our steps. But as it says in an old spiritual, we are to be "like a tree, planted by the waters," a tree that "shall not be moved."

When we're challenged by religious leaders who have forgotten what the covenant of God is all about, we can't let ourselves be intimidated. We have to recognize where the problem is coming from—and then be about the business of breaking free, much as is suggested by a contemporary gospel song entitled "Shake the Devil Off!"

For Discussion: Mark shows us Jesus asking, "How long shall I be with you?" What do you think is the significance of that question?

TEXT TO READ: MARK 9:19 *(last four words)*-20

COMMENT ON THE TEXT: Mark's Jesus interweaves large issues with specific actions. And so, no sooner than Jesus raises the larger issue of faithless behavior, he responds to the specific need. "Bring that troubled son to me," Jesus says.

As soon as they bring the son, another seizure hits his body. He falls on the ground. He rolls around, foaming at the mouth. It's another dreadful convulsion. If the disciples had not been diverted from their mission, if the disciples' faith had not wavered, if the disciples had not been shaken by faithless religious leaders who had too small a view of God's love and God's way, then the son would not have had to experience this additional convulsion. The faithlessness of the scribes, the faithlessness of the disciples, and the faithlessness of the crowd has led to increased suffering. It's as if Mark wants to remind us that faithlessness has consequences—not just for us but for others.

As it says in Malachi 2:5 (NRSV), the covenant of God is "a covenant of life and well-being." When we break faith with that covenant, when we walk in our own way, and when we let others talk us out of doing what needs to be done, real suffering results. Real people are hurt.

TEXT TO READ: MARK 9:21-22

COMMENT ON THE TEXT: For early readers of Mark, these two verses may have helped explain what the scribes were arguing about. Through the dialogue between Jesus and the father, we learn that these seizures are not new. The man's son has suffered them from infancy. Nor are they mild. Sometimes he has been thrown into fire. Sometimes into water. Often the seizures put him at risk of death.

For the scribes, these troubles of the son may have been a sign that he or his parents are horrible sinners, never to be redeemed, never to be freed. In many cultures, troubles that came at birth were wrongly thought to be signs of God's judgment. And to those afflicted with such thinking, the fact that the seizures put the son at the risk of death may have seemed to show an alliance between his parents and the devil.

The scribes, with their false righteousness, may have argued that such a person had no place in God's love. Perhaps they felt such a person was to be excluded, written off, judged, and shunned. Perhaps they couldn't accept the statement in Malachi that no matter who we are, no matter what troubles come upon us, and no matter how others might classify us, one God has created us all. We are all included in God's covenant of life—without distinction, without restriction.

In Mark's telling of the story, the father isn't willing to buy into that kind of thinking. He's seen his son's suffering. In a real sense, he's suffered with him. So on behalf of them both, the father pleads with the disciples for compassion, for healing, for relief. But they "could not." Now he turns to Jesus: "If you, unlike your disciples, if you can do anything for us, please help us. If you are able, have compassion!"

TEXT TO READ: MARK 9:23-24

COMMENT ON THE TEXT: Jesus responds with amazement—and perhaps dismay. He begins by repeating several of the words the man has used. Some of this is obscure in the King James Version, but in effect Jesus looks at this anguished father and says, "Did you really mean to say, 'If you are able'? Don't you know that all things are 'able' to those who believe?"

In effect Jesus reminds the man that only a faithless generation does nothing for those in need. Only a faithless generation believes God's ways cannot be pursued or lived or shared. Those whose faith "shall not be moved"—they are not hindered. They are not bound. They have a covenant from God, "a covenant of life and well-being," a covenant that knows no partiality. Those whose faith does not waver will pursue life and well-being, love and grace, peace and redemption—for all who need it.

On hearing Jesus' words, the man's eyes fill with tears. "I believe!" he cries. "Help my unbelief!" A faithless generation has sometimes caused the faith to slip from him.

For Discussion: To what extent is the father's situation—faith and faithlessness, mixed together—true of us? What are the forces that batter us, diminish our faith, and keep us from acting in God's strong way?

TEXT TO READ: MARK 9:25-27

COMMENT ON THE TEXT: In Mark's dramatic story, the man's troubled son has had a convulsion as he is being brought to Jesus. Now he's rolling on the ground, and a crowd comes running. Mark wants us, like the crowd, to see that it is faithlessness that disables us. It is faithlessness that declares love to be impossible. It is faithlessness that labels peace and forgiveness an impossible ideal. It is faithlessness that says grace is for the deserving. It is faithlessness that incapacitates us, disempowers us.

With the crowd before him, Jesus shows the other way, God's way. He rebukes the spirit that has seized the man's son—and charges that spirit to enter the son "no more." A final convulsion shakes the son, and he falls motionless onto the ground.

The crowd, still not believing, thinks the son is dead. But to dispel any doubt, Jesus takes the son's hand, and the son—whom the scribes are so eager to write off—stands up, on his own accord. The seizures have left him. The faithlessness that led to "could not" has been replaced by a faith that exclaims "why not!"

TEXT TO READ: MARK 9:28-29

COMMENT ON THE TEXT: Later, when they are alone, the disciples ask Jesus why they had not been able to do what he had earlier empowered them to do. And Jesus tells them that "only prayer" drives this kind out.

At first Jesus' comment seems strange. There has been no previous mention of prayer in the story. And there is no mention of praying before Jesus heals the boy. But Jesus' word about prayer reminds us to ask who it is that we're listening to. Are we, like the disciples, being overcome by negative authorities that misunderstand the gospel? Are we having our faith shaken by those who disable rather than enable? Are we being led astray by voices that preach restriction and exclusion? Are we letting the cries of those who proclaim "impossible" keep us from hearing the voice of a God who makes all things new?

Only by staying in tune with God, says Mark, through prayer and regular interaction with the Way Maker, will our courage remain strong. Like the disciples, we live in a faithless generation. But when we drench ourselves in One whose love knows no limits, we are like a tree planted by the water. Storms may rage. Powerful forces may try to quench our hope. But when we anchor our souls in the One whose covenant is "a covenant of life and well-being," we shall not be moved.

On the Mount of Transfiguration, a voice from the cloud said, "This is my Beloved. Listen to him!" This story that follows illustrates why. When we listen to the naysayers, when we tune our ears to those who are trying to keep us from breaking free, all faith slips from us. Suffering increases. And we have no power.

AND HE TOOK A CHILD, AND SET HIM IN THE MIDST OF THEM: AND WHEN HE HAD TAKEN HIM IN HIS ARMS, HE SAID UNTO THEM, WHOSOEVER SHALL RECEIVE ONE OF SUCH CHILDREN IN MY NAME, RECEIVETH ME . . . —MARK 9:36-37

BREAK BREAD TOGETHER ON OUR KNEES

MARK 9:30-40

SETTING THE STAGE

PART ONE: In the preceding verses of Mark, the disciples have been overly influenced by the religious scribes. And because they have been listening to them instead of God, they are unable to heal a young man who is afflicted with violent convulsions. Jesus comes on the scene and refers to the scribes and those who are influenced by them as a "faithless generation." Then Jesus casts out the demon.

But there is more to the story than this because it is filled with allusions to the words of Malachi, where priests and religious leaders are called faithless for failing to uphold the covenant of God. The priests of Malachi's day were showing partiality. They were affirming some people and belittling others. They were failing to remember, says Malachi, that one God created us all. They were forgetting that God's covenant is a "covenant of life and well-being" (Malachi 2:5, NRSV). They were forgetting that all people—regardless of social standing, economic wealth, political power, or anything else—have great worth in God's sight.

PART TWO: The verses from Mark that we look at today build on the verses that have gone before. Jesus will be calling on his disciples to be agents of God's covenant. He will call on them to set aside partiality. He will call on them to set aside pride. He will call on them to honor and treasure all of God's creation. Even those who have no social standing. Even those with no money. Even those with no political or economic power. Even those who seem to be going their own way.

Unfortunately the disciples, like so many of us, are slow to understand. So Jesus will urge them to hurry up. "Get on board, little children," he will tell them, for the consequences of breaking faith with God's covenant are serious indeed.

TEXT TO READ: MARK 9:30-31

COMMENT ON THE TEXT: Jesus has cast out a demon. That demon had been causing a young man to experience terrible convulsions. As the demon comes out, the young man falls to the ground. The crowd thinks he's dead. But Jesus extends a hand, and the young man rises. He's free, no longer bound. A demon sought to destroy him. But the chains of that demon can hold him no more.

Now Jesus takes his disciples and travels quietly through the hills and valleys of Galilee. This is not a time for public ministry. They stick to back roads and quiet lanes. Jesus has seen some dangerous signs in his disciples. They've been listening to the wrong voices. They've been seeing the world through the wrong lenses. Jesus has some important teaching to do. He needs to get their hearts back in the right place.

So he begins by telling his disciples again about what is going to happen to him. He tells them he will be "delivered into the hands of men." The Greek word that Mark uses for "delivered" is a judicial word. It implies being handed over to the legal authorities. And then, says Jesus, he will be "killed." He will be put to death at the hands of those same legal authorities. Capital punishment will be his fate. The state will see him as a dangerous threat, as someone to be eliminated, snuffed out, and destroyed.

Then Jesus tells his disciples that none of that will stop him. He plans to take up his cross and follow. He'll move ahead anyhow. He'll go on serving others, in God's way. It's as if Jesus has heard a call. A call from above. He knows what God's covenant is all about. They'll kill him, sure. They'll ridicule him and exterminate him. But he'll rise again.

For Mark, it's as if Jesus is saying that the demons that rule this land will knock me down. Yes, you'll think I'm dead. So will the multitude. Evil may even dance in glee on my grave. But it won't dance long. Three days, no more. Three days, and then I'll rise. For God will reach down with a mighty hand. And like the young man I just healed, like the young man that the crowd thought was dead, I'll stand.

TEXT TO READ: MARK 9:32

For Discussion: Why do you think Jesus' words were so hard for the disciples to understand? Why do you think they were afraid to ask Jesus what he meant? What parts of the message of Jesus are we afraid to understand? What kinds of things are best understood by and by?

TEXT TO READ: MARK 9:33-34

COMMENT ON THE TEXT: Mark now shows us Jesus and his disciples as they return to Capernaum. This is a familiar place, a home place. It's the setting for many of the early events in the Gospel of Mark. Mark has described it as the hometown of Peter and Andrew, James and John. He implies that some of the other disciples may have been from here as well.

In the safety of a home, in this comfortable and familiar place, Jesus asks the disciples what they were arguing about among themselves on "the way." In the Gospel of Mark, "on the way" always has a kind of double meaning. It refers, in one sense, to being on a journey, traveling down a road. But in a larger sense, it also refers to walking in the way of God. It refers to the new way of living that God has called us to. It involves being faithful to the ways of the Way Maker.

So when Mark shares with us Jesus' question, he wants us to understand it in both senses. He wants us to picture Jesus turning to his disciples and asking them, in the most pointed way, what was it that they were arguing about as they walked with him on the way. Not just what they argued about on the literal road but also what they argued about while they were supposed to be moving forward in God's new way. What was it that they were arguing about as they were supposed to be understanding what it means to be faithful to God's covenant?

With his wonderful sense of drama, Mark then shows us the disciples drawing back from Jesus. They bite their tongues. They clamp their hands over their mouths. They glance quickly at each other, begging each other not to say. And, in the end, no one breathes a word. They don't dare say. They don't dare tell.

But then Mark lets us, his readers, in on the awful secret. The disciples have been arguing among themselves about who is the greatest. They've been competing with each other for places of honor. They've been jockeying with each other for social standing and spiritual prestige. It's as if they haven't heard a thing that Jesus has been saying.

For Discussion: Why are questions about who is the greatest still so important to us? In what ways does the pursuit of social standing and personal honor keep us from walking in the ways of God?

TEXT TO READ: MARK 9:35

COMMENT ON THE TEXT: In Mark's drama, the disciples don't need to answer Jesus' question. For he knows what they're up to. He knows the self-serving desires of their hearts. He knows the prideful longings of their minds.

So Mark shows us Jesus sitting down on the ground, as teachers in that day would do. The disciples, still feeling a bit sheepish, sprawl down on the ground around him.

"If anyone wants to be first in God's eyes," says Jesus, "then that person will need to be last in the world's eyes. For we don't become first by demanding that others serve us or show us respect. We become first in God's eyes by giving ourselves in service to others."

Earlier in Mark, Jesus criticizes Peter for thinking the things of people rather than the things of God. Here too Jesus seems to be saying that the ways of God turn the world upside down. The things that seem to count least are the things that count most.

For Discussion: Can you think of ways in which we who say we follow God fail to abide by the teaching in this passage?

TEXT TO READ: MARK 9:36-37

FIRST COMMENT ON THE TEXT: Jesus and the disciples are at a home in Capernaum. Real people live there, including children. But in this day, young children are seen as insignificant. Until they reach the age when they can work and contribute financially to the well-being of the household, they are not even thought of as having a place on the social ladder. They are so far down that they almost don't count.

Part of this grows out of economics. Young children can't contribute anything. They're a financial drain. And death rates at this time from childhood diseases are much higher than they are now. You never know when a child might die. So it's risky to get too close or too emotionally attached. The old commandment to respect your elders also plays a role. People twist that to mean that the older you are, the more honor you are due. The flip side is that the younger you are, the more worthless you are. No honor is due a child.

In such a context, the scene that Mark paints for us is rather startling. Jesus takes a young child from the household—someone who would be viewed as insignificant and irrelevant—and then Jesus sets that child in the midst of his disciples, in the place that would normally be occupied only by Jesus, their teacher. And then Mark says that Jesus reaches over and embraces the child. He wraps the child in his arms, as people of Jesus' day would hug and greet an honored guest. Through his embrace, Jesus is not just treating the child kindly. He is treating the child as an honored equal. He is demonstrating, through his embrace, the same truth that Malachi proclaimed—the truth that one God created us all. And all have worth in God's eyes.

SECOND COMMENT ON THE TEXT: Jesus' action is a powerful witness to what it means to walk in God's way. But Mark isn't willing to leave it at that. He gives us words from Jesus as well. And those words have an equally radical message, for they embody a logic that is a bit foreign to our normal way of thinking. But it's a logic that comes through again and again in Jesus' teaching. And it's critical to understanding how Mark wants us to live.

After putting his arms around the child, Jesus turns to his disciples and says, "Whoever welcomes a child like this in my name, whoever honors and respects a little child that the world treats as insignificant, is not just welcoming and honoring that child. No," says Jesus, "whoever does a thing like that is welcoming and honoring me." But it doesn't end there. For Jesus continues, saying, "And anyone who welcomes and honors me is welcoming and honoring the One who sent me."

Although the logic of Jesus' argument isn't necessarily natural to us, it isn't hard to understand. Mark is saying that if you welcome and honor a child—or anyone whom the world sees as irrelevant—then you're welcoming Jesus, for Jesus has embraced the child. Jesus has embraced the despised. Jesus has embraced all those that the world casts aside.

And when you welcome and honor Jesus, you welcome and honor God Almighty, for God Almighty has likewise hugged and embraced this one called Jesus. Mark has just taken us up the Mount of Transfiguration, where we saw Jesus wrapped in a holy glow. And then Mark let us hear a voice from a cloud announcing to us that Jesus is God's beloved. Jesus is God's child. So when we welcome and honor Jesus, we welcome and honor the One God who has created us all.

By implication, of course, the reverse is also true. When you dishonor a child—or anyone the world would cast aside—then you dishonor Jesus because you are dishonoring one whom Jesus has embraced. And if you dishonor Jesus, you dishonor God Almighty, because God Almighty has embraced and honored Jesus.

For Discussion: Who are the people who get cast aside today or treated as irrelevant even by people who call themselves Christians? What can we do to better receive and honor those who are demeaned by our world?

TEXT TO READ: MARK 9:38

COMMENT ON THE TEXT: Prior to this, Mark has often presented Peter as the bungling disciple who blurts out the wrong thing at the wrong time. But apparently this tendency wasn't limited to Peter. For in Mark 9:38-39, it's John who shows he has no understanding of what Jesus is saying.

Mark piles the misguided words of John right on top of the deeply profound teaching of Jesus. Mark doesn't want us to miss the irony. Here is Jesus, embracing a child and explaining to his disciples that God's covenant of life and well-being is for all people. Here is Jesus, explaining that when you welcome and embrace those who the world would shut out, you welcome and embrace Jesus. And by welcoming and embracing Jesus, you welcome and embrace the God who created us all.

But it's as if none of this has sunk in for John. For no sooner are Jesus' words out of his mouth than John interrupts to boast of his own unholy action. "Jesus," he says, "we saw somebody casting out devils in your name. But he wasn't of our number. We tried to get him to follow us, but he wouldn't. So we forbade him to cast out any more devils. We told him to stop because he wouldn't take orders from your disciples."

It's as if John is saying to Jesus, "Hey, look what we did! Aren't you proud of us? We stopped that man from casting out devils. He was doing it in your name. But he wouldn't bow before us. He wouldn't honor us as we deserve. Can you imagine that?"

The words of John reveal that the disciples are still stuck in the pursuit of their own honor. They have failed to see that you can't bring honor to yourself without bringing dishonor to others. Here was someone who was healing and helping others—in ways that the disciples themselves had sometimes been unable to do. But because the person wouldn't bow before them, they tried to stop him.

Mark wants us to see that we can dishonor others not just by ignoring them, as children are sometimes ignored. We can also dishonor others by seeking to control them—by holding power over them, ordering them around to make us feel good about ourselves.

BACKGROUND TEXT TO READ: NUMBERS 11:24-29

For Discussion: Who are the people today who God's people wrongly forbid from doing what God would have them do, simply because they don't fit into our pattern or don't fall under our control?

TEXT TO READ: MARK 9:39-40

FIRST COMMENT ON THE TEXT: John tells Jesus that he and the others have forbidden an exorcist from casting out any more devils in Jesus' name. Jesus' response is stern and direct. "Don't forbid him!" says Jesus. "That man may not be walking with me. That man may not be walking with you. But he's doing what God wants done. He understands that to be first in the eyes of God you must be give yourself in service to others, which you yourselves have not yet understood!"

Then Mark shows us Jesus saying something rather ominous, the full meaning of which will not be clear until later in the story. "After all," says Jesus, "someone who does a miracle in my name—someone who reaches out if needed to and embraces those who are hurting—such a one will not lightly speak evil of me."

There is an implied contrast in Jesus' words. It isn't stated. But it's implied so strongly we can almost hear it. "Unlike you," Jesus seems to say, "such a one knows what mercy is about. Unlike you, such a one fully embraces those I embrace. Unlike you, such a one will not deny me or belittle me or betray me when the going gets rough."

Then Jesus sums up the truth: "Whoever is not against us is for us."

For Discussion: What does it mean for us, in today's world, to know that whoever is not against us is for us?

SECOND COMMENT ON THE TEXT: According to some historians, U.S. plantation owners introduced Christianity to their slaves in the naive hope that it would make their slaves passive and obedient. In practice, however, it often had the opposite effect. Many slaves found in the message of Jesus a message of liberation and hope.

Seeing what was happening, plantation owners often tried to control the faith of their slaves. Like the disciples, they tried to forbid those they couldn't control. Slaves were ordered not to meet on their own for worship. But many went right on meeting—secretly. In shady woods or hidden fields, they would drop to their knees and worship a God who welcomed and respected them as the world would not.

Today we often think of the old spiritual "Let Us Break Bread Together" as a communion song. But according to some historians, in slave days it was sung as a way of communicating from one person to another that it was meeting time. It was a song of dignity and a song of defiance. It was a signal that the time had come to slip away from those who showed no mercy. Early in the morning, "with my face to the rising sun," folk would gather to praise the Lord who embraced them, the Lord who always had "mercy on me."

In the verses we looked at today, Mark explores what it means to be faithful to God's covenant. God's way, he declares, is always a way of welcoming—and not forbidding—for the same God has made us all.

SESSION 12

AND HE TOOK
THEM UP IN HIS
ARMS, PUT HIS
HANDS UPON
THEM, AND
BLESSED THEM.
—MARK 10:16

NOT A FRIEND
LIKE THE LOWLY JESUS

MARK 9:41-10:16

Group leaders: This session, because of the interrelated nature of its biblical texts, is longer than most. If you are using this material as a group Bible study and if your time is strictly limited, you may need to break this session in half, even though you will thereby lose some important interconnections. If you have to do that, a good place to stop is just before reading Mark 10:1.

SETTING THE STAGE

In Mark's telling of the story, Jesus has caught the disciples arguing about which of them is the greatest. He tells them that you don't get to be the greatest by honoring yourself. Rather, you get to be the greatest by giving yourself in service to others. The one who is "servant of all" is the one who is first in God's eyes.

Jesus and his disciples are meeting together in a home in Capernaum, a familiar place for all of them near the Sea of Galilee. And while they're talking, Jesus startles the disciples even further. He brings a child into their midst—a child who, in Jesus' day, is often thought of as nothing, an insignificant being, a kind of person-in-waiting with zero status, zero value. Jesus takes the child into his arms. He embraces the child with the kind of bear hug that is typically offered in that day when you are meeting a close friend of equal standing.

Then Jesus declares that anyone who welcomes and embraces a child such as this is welcoming and embracing Jesus. The logic is simple. I've hugged and embraced this child, says Jesus. So when you welcome and embrace someone with zero social standing, like this child whom I've embraced, then you're also embracing me. And when you embrace me, you're also embracing God Almighty, the Maker of us all, for God Almighty has embraced me. It's a matter of going from hug . . . to hug . . . to hug.

But the disciples, as Mark portrays them, aren't ready to listen. They're stuck in old ways of thinking. So John interrupts Jesus and boasts of having forbidden someone from casting out devils in Jesus' name because that person wouldn't give honor and glory to the disciples. The person wasn't following the disciples and doing what they commanded. The person wouldn't bow under their control.

Jesus is appalled, and he sternly orders the disciples to "forbid him not." The way of God, Jesus seems to be saying, involves welcoming others, not forbidding them. It involves treasuring others, not restricting them. It involves lifting up your neighbors, whoever they might be, not undercutting them or treating them as scum.

TEXT TO READ: MARK 9:41

COMMENT ON THE TEXT: We're still in the remarkable scene that Mark has sketched for us. Jesus and the disciples are visiting together in a home. Perhaps Mark wants us to imagine little children running around, laughing, playing, wondering what's happening.

Then Jesus calls one of the children to him. The child is startled and surprised. Jesus hugs and embraces her in a manner normally reserved for adults. He isn't ignoring her. She's amazed. And in our mind's eye, as Jesus and the disciples talk, we perhaps see other children, eyes wide, peeking around the corner. In time, others dare to join the circle. Jesus' arms reach wide. Each is welcomed. Each is embraced.

Now Jesus turns to these children and addresses them directly. "Truly I tell you," he says, "whoever gives despised and ignored ones like you a cup of water to drink will have a great reward. You may be children. You may be thought of as nothing. You may have no social standing, no economic wealth, no political power, no education, no skills. In the world's eyes, you are least of all. But you've been embraced by me. So you bear my name. You belong to the one they call Messiah. And whoever honors you, even with a cup of cold water, honors me. And when they honor me, they honor God Almighty, the Creator of us all. And all who honor God are due a great reward."

For the disciples, such words are shocking. They have been arguing over who is the greatest. Now Jesus tells them that God's reward goes to those who the world considers nothing. The disciples have been thinking that they are pretty special. After all, don't they bear the name of the one who they follow? Aren't they Jesus' disciples? But now Jesus addresses these little children and tells them that it is they—these supposedly worthless children—who truly bear his name.

For Discussion: Who are the children of our day, the ones our society treats as worthless? Are we willing to believe that ones such as these bear Jesus' name? What forms might "a cup of water" take in our day? What is this "reward" that Jesus is talking about?

TEXT TO READ: MARK 9:42

COMMENT ON THE TEXT: In Mark's drama, it's as if Jesus is now turning again to the disciples. He's giving them the flip side of what he's just told the children. And as Jesus looks his disciples in the eye, it's almost as if he is looking us in the eye as well.

"Remember this," he says, "whoever offends one of these little ones—whoever fails to honor one of these individuals that society thinks of as nothing—it would be better for that person if a huge millstone were hanged about that person's neck and the person were cast into the sea!"

These are frightening words. Jesus isn't playing games. And the image he offers is about as horrible as any disciple could ever imagine. In Jesus' day, grain is ground by millstones. Some are smaller in size and can be turned by a strong individual with bulging muscles. But other millstones are so large that only a donkey can turn them. And the word that Mark uses in this verse is literally the word for a millstone so large that only a strong animal can turn it. This is a huge, heavy stone with a hole in the center.

Jesus tells the disciples that anyone who demeans the honor of one whom Jesus has honored is in serious trouble. You'd be better off, he says, if one of those monster millstones that only a donkey can turn were fitted over your neck and you were thrown into the sea.

To understand the horror of Jesus' image we also need to understand that Jews of Jesus' day, when they die, feel a deep desire to be buried in the earth from which they came. To die at sea, with your body never recovered and your flesh never laid to rest, is about as horrible a thing as anyone can imagine. And yet Jesus is saying that such a fate is better than the fate you will receive if you fail to honor those whom God has honored.

For Discussion: Why do you think Jesus is so vigorous about this, so uncompromising, so frightening? What are the times during history when Jesus might have felt worst about how Christians behaved? When might he have felt best?

BACKGROUND TEXT TO READ: MARK 6:1-3

COMMENT ON THE TEXT: In Mark 6, Jesus and the disciples visit Nazareth, the little town that Jesus calls home. The people in Nazareth ridicule Jesus. Who is he to be doing such things, they ask. He's just a carpenter—no more. He doesn't have a legitimate father. He's just the bastard son of Mary. In our eyes, they say, he's nothing. Mark 6 says that they "took offense" at him.

The word that Mark 6 uses to describe how the people of Nazareth are offended at Jesus is the same word that Mark 9 uses to describe those who "offend" one of the "little ones" whom God has honored and embraced. In some translations, this word is rendered as "stumbling block" or as "to cause one of these little ones to stumble." But in the most literal sense, the word means "to scandalize." Literally, the people of Nazareth are scandalized by Jesus. They see him as a sinner. They see him as worthless. They see him as a nobody whose worthlessness will rub off on them if they aren't careful. So they turn their backs on him. And Jesus finds himself treated "without honor" by the very people who should have treasured him most.

In the same way, Jesus warns his disciples not to scandalize the little ones of this world. He understands, from his experience, how we treat those whom we think of as nothing. We blame them for their sins. We blame them for their weakness. We blame them for their misery. We scandalize them and treat them as worthless. And thereby we cause them to stumble. We take away their dignity. We take away their worth. Instead of treating them as sisters and brothers, we make them bend low, almost to the ground.

Mark presents Jesus as one who understands what it means to be written off. This same understanding comes through in an old spiritual in which the singer expresses the pain of those who feel the world turning its back on them:

> *I met my brother the other day, gave him my right hand.*
> *But just as soon as ever my back was turned,*
> *He took an' scandalize my name!*
> *You call that a brother? No, no! You call that a sister? No, no!*
> *You call that a preacher? No, no! Scandalize my name!*

For Discussion: What are some of the ways that we might be scandalizing the name of God's little ones without even realizing it?

TEXT TO READ: MARK 9:43,45,47-48

(If verses 44 and 46 appear in your Bible, it's best to skip them, since they are probably not original parts of Mark.)

For Discussion: What is Jesus trying to say? Is he literally suggesting that we cut off our hands or pull out our eyes? How do these verses relate to what's gone before?

FIRST COMMENT ON THE TEXT: At this point in the story, Mark shows us Jesus making three similar statements. One is about hands, one about feet, one about eyes. Mark says that if your hand or foot or eye causes you to stumble, then you ought to cut it off or pull it out.

In Mark's day, "hands" and "feet" and "eyes" are sometimes used as a kind of shorthand code, referring to different ways that people could violate the dignity and integrity of their neighbor. Violations of the hand include fraud and forgery—in other words, taking advantage of someone through false writing. Violations of the foot include robbery and persistent theft—in other words, running off with your neighbor's goods. Violations of the eye include adultery and sexual abuse of others—in other words, lusting after someone and then acting on that, no matter who is hurt or brought low in the process.

Through violations of the hand or foot or eye, you could dishonor your neighbor. You could treat your neighbor as worthless. You could devalue those whom God had created, those whom God had embraced, those whom God had welcomed into the human family.

By including these comments, Mark seems to be saying that when we sin against others—when we bring others low—we sin not only against our neighbor but also against God. When we dishonor others, we dishonor God. And in the view of Mark, that's not something any of us should do lightly. It would be better not to have that hand, not to have that foot, not to have that eye if it is going to lead us astray.

For Discussion: In our time, who do you think is more likely to violate their neighbor—those who think of themselves as the greatest or those who think of themselves as "last of all, and servant of all"?

SECOND COMMENT ON THE TEXT: In these verses, Mark presents Jesus saying to his disciples that it would be better for them to lose a hand or a foot or an eye than to dishonor their neighbor and be cast into hell.

The word that is usually translated here as "hell" doesn't mean hell as we usually think of it. The Greek word that is used in these verses is *Gehenna*. And in Mark's day, Gehenna meant the local garbage dump. It was a disgusting, foul-smelling place in which trash rotted and fires burned night and day in an effort to dispose of unwanted waste. It was about as repulsive a place as you could imagine, a place where people dumped garbage and all kinds of human and animal waste.

So what Jesus is saying is that those who demean their neighbor—those who violate their neighbor through hand or foot or eye—all they are fit for is to be cast into Gehenna, that disgusting, smelly place where people dump those things that no longer have any value. In other words, it doesn't matter how great you think you are, for if you've dishonored your neighbor, all you're fit for is the garbage dump.

For Mark, the key question is not what we are worth in the eyes of the world but what we are worth in the eyes of God.

For Discussion: In what ways does this teaching fit or not fit with the teaching in the previous chapter, where Jesus says, "Those who want to save their life will lose it, and those who lose their life for my sake . . . will save it" (Mark 8:35, NRSV)? All of us, if we're honest about it, have sometimes, whether consciously or unconsciously, fallen short of what God expects of us. Does this passage mean we're all going to hell? Do you think Jesus meant to be as harsh as he sounds?

THIRD COMMENT ON THE TEXT: The early readers of Mark's Gospel were deeply familiar with the writings of the Jewish prophets, and Mark loves to word his story in a way that will give his readers bursts of insight. And one of those places is in this passage, where Gehenna, the garbage dump, is described as a place where the "worm dieth not, and the fire is not quenched."

To us, that sounds horrible enough. But for early readers of the Gospel, it would have also been a reminder of the last two verses of the Book of Isaiah, which contain a vivid description of the fate of those who transgress against their neighbor and thus against God.

BACKGROUND TEXT TO READ: ISAIAH 66:23-24

COMMENT ON THE TEXT: As we will soon see, the last two verses of Mark 9 are filled with references to salt. Modern readers sometimes pass over these verses with only a vague understanding of what they mean.

In our day, we tend to think of salt as something that enhances the flavor of foods. Or we think of it as a preservative. But to understand these verses, we have to remember that for Jews of Mark's day, salt is a sign of God's covenant. Salt is a sign of the holy agreement that binds God and God's people together. Salt is a sign of loving fellowship, a sign that two parties have linked their fortunes together. For this reason, the Jewish people were commanded to sprinkle salt over their sacrifices. Salt was a required element of any acceptable sacrifice to God.

BACKGROUND TEXTS TO READ:
LEVITICUS 2:13; 2 CHRONICLES 13:5; EZEKIEL 43:23-24

TEXT TO READ: MARK 9:49-50A

COMMENT ON THE TEXT: Mark 9:49 comes across a bit differently in different translations, partly because some of the older manuscripts of Mark vary in how it's worded. But essentially Mark 9:49 seems to be a reminder that with every sacrifice made to God, with every sacrifice made over fire, salt is required.

Salt is a sign of God's covenant, a covenant that Malachi describes as "a covenant of life and well-being" (Malachi 2:5, NRSV). So in Mark 9:50, Mark presents Jesus as reminding his disciples that "salt is good." And yet, says Jesus, "If salt loses its saltiness, how can you can get that saltiness back?" The answer is that you can't. It's gone. Salt without saltiness is no longer able to do what it was meant to do.

Perhaps what Mark is trying to convey to us is that in the eyes of Jesus, all of us are salt. We who follow Jesus are to be more than an empty sign of the covenant. We are to be salty through and through. And we are to make holy the sacrifice of Jesus by treating all of God's little ones with honor and respect.

The flip side of this is that if we dishonor others by pursuing our own greatness and if we ignore those whom the world sees as worthless, then we will lose our saltiness. We'll become good for nothing—except the garbage dump.

An old spiritual expresses the same perspective:

> *You say you're aiming for the skies?*
> *You must be loving at God's command.*
> *Why don't you quit your telling lies?*
> *You must be loving at God's command.*
> *You say the Lord has set you free?*
> *You must be loving at God's command.*
> *Why don't you let your neighbor be?*
> *You must be loving at God's command.*
> *You seek God's grace but don't seek right—*
> *you must be loving at God's command!*

TEXT TO READ: MARK 9:50B

COMMENT ON THE TEXT: Mark wraps up this scene with a direct command from Jesus. It's a single command said two ways.

First, Jesus looks at his disciples and says, "Have salt in yourselves." In effect Jesus is saying, don't lose your saltiness. Be a strong sign of God's covenant of life and well-being. Don't become worthless. Then Jesus repeats himself and says the same thing another way. "Be at peace one with another." In other words, when we're living as salt, when we're truly a sign of God's covenant, we will be at peace with all people.

We won't dishonor others. We won't forbid others. We won't put others down. We'll treasure each person we meet. No matter how broken they might appear. No matter how worthless or small the world might say they are. And no matter how much we'd like to control them. Nor will we ever scandalize another's name. For as the prophet Malachi said, "One God has created us all."

The ways of the world are ways of violence. Pushing ourselves to the top means pushing someone else down. The arrogance of the world is an assault, both on God and on God's little ones, the weak, the poor, the ridiculed, the hungry, and the imprisoned. Mark sees the message of Jesus as a plea to each of us to "lay down" our sword and shield and "study war no more." Or, in the words of an ancient prayer commonly attributed to St. Francis of Assisi, our request to God should always be, "Make me an instrument of thy peace . . ."

Note: If you are breaking this session in half due to time constraints, this is the place to stop. When you resume, you can reestablish the context by first rereading the previous section in Mark 9:41-50.

TEXT TO READ: MARK 10:1

COMMENT ON THE TEXT: So far, most of Mark has been set in Galilee or in the predominantly Gentile areas to the north or west of Galilee. But now Mark takes us on a journey. He shows us Jesus and the disciples leaving their home territory. They travel to Judea and the areas on the far side of the Jordan River.

This new area is significant for several reasons. One, Judea is where John the Baptist did his baptizing (Mark 1:4-5). Two, Judea is where Jesus was tested by Satan and ministered to by angels (Mark 1:13). And three, Judea is where Herod Antipas rules. This is the Herod who chopped off the head of John the Baptist after John spoke against the arrogant way in which Herod had stolen his brother's wife, even though his brother hadn't divorced her (Mark 6:14-29).

Now, as Jesus enters Judea and the area around the Jordan, Mark tells us that crowds of people surround him. They want to hear Jesus' words. They want to feel his touch. They want to experience his love.

TEXT TO READ: MARK 10:2

For Discussion: Who is it that comes to Jesus? What is it that they ask? What does Mark say they are doing to Jesus by their question? Why do you think Mark considers this question a temptation?

FIRST COMMENT ON THE TEXT: In Jesus' day, there were two schools of thought about what constituted the proper circumstances for a man to divorce his wife. Some religious leaders took one view. Some took another. But in Mark's drama, the Pharisees don't ask Jesus which view he sides with. They ask, "Is it lawful for a man to divorce his wife?" In other words, the Pharisees are asking Jesus if it is consistent with God's will for a man to divorce his wife, assuming the right circumstances exist.

Mark tells us that by asking this question, the Pharisees are "tempting" Jesus. Some translations say that the Pharisees are "testing" Jesus, but the meaning is the same. And at first, the description of this question as a test or a temptation might seem strange. What is there about this question that tests Jesus' commitment to the ways of God?

But the wording of the question in the King James Version is revealing and helps us understand what is at issue here. Yes, the question is about divorce. But more specifically, in the words of the King James Version, it's about whether or not it's right "for a man to put away his wife." In short, this is a question about the mentality of exclusion. It's a continuation of the same theme that Mark has been presenting in verse after verse, in paragraph after paragraph.

The temptation is the mentality of exclusion. The Pharisees are probing to see how far Jesus is willing to go. Will he accept the ways of the world, in which one person considers himself or herself greater than others—or will he hold to the ways of God, in which all people have equal worth, in which no one is to be shut out or put away?

SECOND COMMENT ON THE TEXT: In Palestine during Jesus' day, as in so many other places, divorce is available only to men. A few bigger cities, like Rome, are beginning to let women initiate divorce. But in most places, including Palestine, it is the exclusive right of the man.

In the eyes of those who think of themselves as the greatest, women don't count for anything. Women are at the mercy of men, and most men don't show mercy. Women are second class—or worse. They are excluded from the circles of power, socially, politically, and economically.

If a man doesn't like the woman he is married to or if he finds her an economic burden, he puts her away. He writes her off. He sends her on her way. And in Jesus' day, a divorced woman quickly finds herself in poverty, hunger, and despair. Most men don't care. They have the mentality of exclusion. They write off anybody they feel like writing off. They have forgotten God's covenant of life and well-being. They have forgotten that one God has created us all.

For Discussion: How is divorce similar or different today?

TEXT TO READ: MARK 10:3-4

COMMENT ON THE TEXT: With his wonderful sense of drama, Mark shows us Jesus and the Pharisees bantering together about divorce. And we discover that instead of directly answering the Pharisees' question, Jesus turns around and asks them "what Moses commanded."

We can almost see a twinkle in Mark's eye as he develops this story, for Jesus' question is loaded. When we listen closely, we discover that Jesus never says, "Tell me what Moses commanded about divorce." He says, "Tell me what Moses commanded." No topic is mentioned.

But the Pharisees don't listen closely, so they quickly fall into the trap. They answer as if Jesus' question is about divorce. After all, that's the topic they have been addressing. So they say, "Moses allowed a man to write a certificate of dismissal and put his woman out." In other words, say the Pharisees, Moses lets men treat their wives as worthless. The effects of the divorce on the wife don't matter. After all, according to their way of thinking, a wife is only a woman.

For Discussion: By their easy acceptance of divorce, for the man only, what sort of attitude are the Pharisees demonstrating?

BACKGROUND TEXT TO READ: DEUTERONOMY 24:1

COMMENT ON THE TEXT: The first four verses of Deuteronomy 24 seem to outline a scenario for divorce, and in Jesus' day, these verses have become the basis for the Jewish rules of divorce. Jewish commentators of the time sometimes argue over what circumstances are appropriate or inappropriate for divorce, but always there is an assumption that divorce is only for the man. The woman doesn't matter. And it's this mentality of exclusion that Jesus is about to jump on, for in Jesus' eyes, such a mentality violates the ways of God.

TEXT TO READ: MARK 10:5

COMMENT ON THE TEXT: In this verse, Mark shows us that not everything recorded in Scripture reflects the ways of God. Deuteronomy 24 may be historically accurate in the sense that the people of God did set up a system that allowed men and only men to initiate divorce. But according to Jesus, says Mark, this provision is built on the mentality of exclusion. It reflects a "hardness of heart," not the heart of God.

When Jesus asks the Pharisees, "What did Moses command you?" he is asking the Pharisees to grasp not a specific teaching that may have grown out of wrong motives. Rather, Jesus wants the Pharisees to see the heart and soul of Moses' teaching, for the heart and soul of Moses' teaching reflects the abiding ways of God. The heart and soul of Moses' teaching reflects the covenant of God, a covenant of life and well-being that sees each of us as created by one God. And it is this creation theme that Jesus is about to turn to.

TEXT TO READ: MARK 10:6

For Discussion: What truths does Jesus point to in this verse? How do these truths undercut the mentality of exclusion and make irrelevant the question of who is the greatest?

TEXT TO READ: MARK 10:7-8

For Discussion: What points does Jesus seem to be making? How do these points undercut the mentality of exclusion?

TEXT TO READ: MARK 10:9

For Discussion: Do you think that Jesus is talking here about something bigger than divorce? If so, what point is this verse trying to make? What role do you think it is playing in the overall argument?

COMMENT ON THE TEXT: In these verses, Jesus lifts up a fundamental principle. He draws that principle from patterns established at "the beginning of the creation." In effect Jesus is telling the Pharisees that they can't see the forest for the trees. They're focused on a tiny detail that reflects historical reality but does not reflect the divine will of God.

The truth that Jesus holds up goes back to the early chapters of Genesis, where God creates both male and female. Both male and female are products of God's hand. So one is not greater than the other. Neither male nor female can be worthless in God's eyes because God creates them both.

Further, according to Genesis, a man who marries does not remain with his father and mother. Rather, he will "cleave" to his wife. They are bonded, one to another. No more is it two separate, independent people who go their own ways, pursue their own goals, and seek individual greatness. Rather, the two become "one flesh." Together they become a new entity, a new creation. And if they are one flesh, then one isn't better than the other. Nor can one partner exclude or abuse or demean the other as if the other is not important. There's an essential wholeness, the text seems to say, a wholeness that links men and women together.

In Mark's drama, Jesus then sums up his argument by stating a general principle. In many ways, it's a principle that underlies all that Jesus has said about the horrors of exclusion. "What God hath joined together," Jesus declares, "let not man put asunder." In other words, if God has created us all and if we all have been hugged and embraced by this same God, then anyone who tries to put away one of God's own is in great peril, for such a one is trying to undo what God has done. Such a one is not only scandalizing the name of another but also is slapping the face of God Almighty. And, as it suggests in Mark 9:43, it might be better for such people to put a huge millstone around their neck and jump into the deepest part of the sea.

For Discussion: In Mark's day, one of the ways that women are put down and treated like dirt is through the divorce laws. In what ways are women today still victims of exclusion?

TEXT TO READ: MARK 10:10

COMMENT ON THE TEXT: The disciples, as usual, don't get it. They think in human ways rather than in divine ways. The mentality of exclusion runs deep in their souls. So when they get alone with Jesus, in the safety of a home, they ask him again about what he was saying. They don't understand. It's not so much that the words are baffling to them. Rather, it's that Jesus looks at the world in a whole new way.

For Discussion: How do you think Jesus feels when the disciples again reveal their lack of understanding? When the disciples ask Jesus the question that's on their mind, do they show themselves to be dumb or show themselves to be smart? Why?

TEXT TO READ: MARK 10:11

COMMENT ON THE TEXT: If the disciples were baffled before, they're really baffled now, for Jesus says something out of the ordinary for his day. He says that any man who divorces his wife and marries another is committing adultery against the first woman he married.

In Jesus' day, it's thought that only women can commit adultery. Men do what they want, but when women do the same, it's adultery. Now Jesus is saying that a man who casts aside one wife and takes another commits adultery. Such an act, Jesus says, is an act of violence against a woman. And each woman has worth. She has been created by God, just like the man. She and the man are one flesh.

Mark wants us to realize that the mentality of exclusion is the mentality of violence. We are supposed to be salt poured onto sacrificial service of others. And when we are truly salt, according to Mark 9:50, we are "at peace one with another." We don't exclude. We don't demean. We don't step on others.

In Jesus' day, as in ours, the violence of exclusion happens all too often. One way it happens is through an arrogant, man-centered style of divorce. Mark shows us Jesus trying to put a stop to that. To use the words of an old song, Mark wants us to see that when it comes to victims of assault, "there's not a friend like the lowly Jesus."

TEXT TO READ: MARK 10:12

COMMENT ON THE TEXT: Mark pushes his readers at every turn. First he shocks them with Jesus' statement about the violence of men against women. But now he startles them again by suggesting that if a woman were to divorce her husband, which is unheard of at the time, then she too would be committing adultery. She too would be practicing the violence of exclusion.

Perhaps Mark includes this parallel teaching because he wants us to remember the overall point: Any time we cast aside another human being, any time we act with arrogance instead of humility, we are failing to walk in the ways of God, whose loving embrace knows no end.

TEXT TO READ: MARK 10:13-14

COMMENT ON THE TEXT: So that we won't miss the larger point he is trying to make, Mark returns to the children with which he began this sequence of scenes. People are bringing children to Jesus. This isn't surprising, for in Mark, the crowd often seems to understand better than the disciples. But once again, the disciples rebuke them. The disciples think that children are too small, too insignificant, too unimportant to take up Jesus' time. But when Jesus sees what's happening, he's "much displeased." The disciples have blown it again.

"Let the little ones come to me," he says, "and forbid them not, for the kingdom of God belongs to such as these."

TEXT TO READ: MARK 10:15-16

COMMENT ON THE TEXT: These two verses are a two-edged sword. On the one hand, we see Jesus taking into his lap the very people his disciples wanted to exclude. His love is a blessing. On the other hand, we also see Jesus issuing a stern warning. Anyone who rejects or excludes, he says, has no place in the kingdom of God. Turn your back on one of the world's little ones, and you've turned your back on God.

An old hymn says, "Come, thou fount of every blessing, tune my heart to sing thy grace." The Gospel of Mark is pleading with us to tune not just our hearts but all of our lives to "streams of mercy, never ceasing." Mark wants us singing, "O to grace, how great a debtor, daily I'm constrained to be! Let thy goodness, like a fetter, bind my wandering heart to thee!"

AND WHEN HE
WAS GONE FORTH
INTO THE WAY,
THERE CAME
ONE RUNNING,
AND KNEELED
TO HIM, AND
ASKED HIM,
GOOD MASTER,
WHAT SHALL
I DO THAT I
MAY INHERIT
ETERNAL LIFE?
—MARK 10:17

IN ZION, THE BEAUTIFUL CITY OF GOD

MARK 10:13-31

Group leaders: This session, because of the interrelated nature of its biblical texts, is longer than most. If you are using this material as a group Bible study and if your time is strictly limited, you may need to break this session in half, even though you will thereby lose some important interconnections. If you have to do that, a good place to stop is just before reading Mark 10:22.

SETTING THE STAGE

In scene after scene, Mark has been reminding us of the human tendency to build ourselves up while putting others down. At the beginning of this series of scenes, Jesus catches the disciples arguing among themselves about who is the greatest. It's a mentality we all share—a mentality of putting great gulfs between ourselves and others. Jesus' response to this is to tell his disciples that if they want to be great in God's eyes, then they must become servants of all people. In other words, we must break the walls that we put between ourselves and others. We must bridge the gap. We must reach out to others, as if they and we are one.

To reinforce his point, Jesus embraces a child and explains that those who are seen as little in the eyes of the world are still great in God's eyes. Mark includes other examples as well, including women, who, in his day, are seen as little more than the property of their husbands. Mark reminds his readers that women too are to be treated with dignity. We are to honor and respect all people. God's covenant, Mark reminds us, is a covenant of life and well-being for all people, and we are to live as if we are the salt, or finishing touch, of that covenant.

TEXT TO READ: MARK 10:13-14

COMMENT ON THE TEXT: People have heard that Jesus is different. He doesn't dismiss those that the world sees as irrelevant. He doesn't turn his back on those the world sees as too small to matter. So people bring children to Jesus, little ones who, in that day, were thought of as nothing.

The fumbling disciples try to stop people from bringing their children. When Jesus discovers what the disciples are doing, he orders them to let the little ones come to him. And then he gives the reason—and the reason is important for understanding the next scene in Mark.

In the words of the King James Version, Jesus tells his disciples that "of such is the kingdom of God." The New Revised Standard Version says, "It is to such as these that the kingdom of God belongs." In other words, the kingdom of God is found in the realm of little ones. It is among those whom the world rejects that God's will is honored, that God's way is treasured. And if you want to enter the kingdom of God, you need to enter into the lives of those whom the world considers least.

Mark is saying that those who the disciples forbid to come to Jesus are royal offspring of the Mighty One, for "of such is the kingdom of God." They have position and status in that realm over which God rules.

For Discussion: What difference would it make in our behavior if we believed that the kingdom of God belongs to those people the world considers too small and insignificant to matter? What does this teaching say about the great gulf that some people put between themselves and others?

TEXT TO READ: MARK 10:15

COMMENT ON THE TEXT: Mark shows us Jesus turning to his disciples and telling them that whoever "shall not receive the kingdom of God as a little child" shall not enter that kingdom. Such a person will have no place in that realm where God's will is supreme.

For Discussion: What is this verse saying? Who are the ones who will never enter the kingdom of God? Is the verse saying that you must still be a little child or act like a little child to receive the kingdom of God? Or is it saying something else?

COMMENT ON THE TEXT: This verse is often misinterpreted. And it's easy to misinterpret. When you take its words out of context, it's easy to imagine that the phrase "as a little child" refers to a person who seeks to enter the kingdom of God. Misinterpreted, the verse sounds like, "If you want to receive the kingdom of God, you must be a little child." We know it could not mean that literally, so we say, "Well, that means we must have the attitude and simplicity of a little child."

But that doesn't make sense with what's gone before. Jesus has just said that the kingdom of God belongs to the little ones whom the world casts off. That's where the kingdom of God is. So the phrase "as a little child" does not refer to the one who is seeking to enter the kingdom. Rather, it refers to the kingdom. What Jesus is saying is that when we receive a little child or anyone whom the world has cast off, we are not just receiving a rejected one. Rather, we are entering the kingdom of God. In welcoming and affirming those who the world despises, we enter that place where God is to be found. It is here, among those whom the world has cast off, that the loving hand of God will be seen. It is here that we truly find power and grace. It is here that we demonstrate through our actions that we are indeed breaking free from the world's way of behaving.

TEXT TO READ: MARK 10:16-17

FIRST COMMENT ON THE TEXT: With deliberate intensity, Mark shows us Jesus taking children into his arms, putting his hands on them, and blessing them. Then, as soon as Jesus steps outside, someone comes running up to him with an urgent question. Mark is a master of irony, and he wants us, his readers, to connect these two scenes in our minds.

In this new scene, a man kneels before Jesus and asks what he should do to "inherit eternal life." But even as he asks that question, Mark wants us to remember Jesus, in the previous scene, explaining that whoever wants to enter the kingdom of God must welcome, honor, and receive those whom the world has cast off. The gulfs that we dig between ourselves and others must be bridged.

For Discussion: Look at all the details in Mark 10:17. What are the things about this verse that strike you as interesting? What do you think Mark means to convey by these details?

SECOND COMMENT ON THE TEXT: The man who comes running up to Jesus is a man in a hurry. Perhaps Mark wants us to see him as someone who is overly taken with his own importance, someone whose time is too valuable to waste.

Perhaps there's also a bit of comedy here. The man comes running up to Jesus, panting and out of breath. He's in a dreadful hurry to find out what he has to do to inherit a life that is everlasting, a life that knows no end.

The man kneels and addresses Jesus as "Good Master." Perhaps Mark wants us to see this man as someone for whom social status is all-important. The man kneels and puts Jesus on a pedestal. His mentality is not one of building bridges. It's one of digging gulfs. His is the false humility of one who elevates others because that's also what he wants others to do for him.

THIRD COMMENT ON THE TEXT: This man doesn't come to pay Jesus his respects. He has something he wants. Perhaps this is a man that is used to being on the receiving end of things. And he's heard talk of something good that comes from God that he wants to be sure he's going to receive.

We aren't told what prompts the man's question, but perhaps it grows out of a reading of Daniel 12:2, where the text says, "Many of those who sleep in the dust of the earth shall awake, some to everlasting life" (NRSV). And perhaps Mark is trying to tell us that this man wants to be among the privileged who awake to eternal life. He doesn't want to miss out.

But in Jesus' day, to "inherit eternal life" wouldn't necessarily mean to experience life after death. Devout Jews understood eternal life to be something that begins in the present. To have eternal life means that your life, right now, is blessed by God, the Eternal One. To have eternal life means that you have been accepted into the circle of the righteous. In short, it means something similar to what Jesus means when he talks about entering the kingdom of God. It means that you have been touched by the Eternal, that you are living in God's way, and that you are experiencing God as the true guide and director of your life.

TEXT TO READ: MARK 10:18

For Discussion: Has Jesus answered the man's question? What is Jesus responding to? In what ways does Jesus' response connect to the larger themes of Mark?

COMMENT ON THE TEXT: The man who kneels at Jesus' feet calls Jesus "Good Master" or "Good Teacher." This is an unusual term in Jewish literature. But it's clearly intended to be taken as a term of respect. The man is imparting a high degree of social status to Jesus. And Jesus is not a person who takes kindly to social status. Social status is too often built on the mentality of exclusion, a mentality that says some people are more worthy than others. This same mentality caused the disciples to forbid children from approaching Jesus. They didn't consider the children worthy of his time.

So immediately Jesus challenges the man's use of this title. For it is a title that divides. "There is no one who is good," says Jesus, "except God." Jesus is saying, "Don't go digging gulfs between people. Don't go saying that some matter and some don't, for we have all been created by the same God." Through his words, Jesus challenges the mentality that lies behind much of the world's social structures.

For Discussion: In what ways do we use titles, or a selective lack of titles, to divide people into classes? What difference would it make in our society if we believed that no one is good but God?

BACKGROUND TEXT TO READ: DEUTERONOMY 15:7-11

TEXT TO READ: MARK 10:19

COMMENT ON THE TEXT: Jesus now returns to the man's original question. He begins by reciting some of the basic commandments, particularly those that concern our relationships with others. All of these commands—except one—come from the Ten Commandments.

The one exception is the command to "defraud not." Typically, in Jewish literature, this command is applied primarily to the rich. It is a reminder that the rich are not to withhold the wages of poor laborers who work for them. Employers are to be fair and generous with those who work for them. And wages are to be paid promptly.

BACKGROUND TEXT TO READ: DEUTERONOMY 24:14-15

TEXT TO READ: MARK 10:20

COMMENT ON THE TEXT: In Mark's drama, the man listens to Jesus reciting some of the core commandments, particularly those that address how we are to relate to others. After hearing the list, the man says, "Master, I have kept all these commandments since I was a youth!"

Mark portrays this fellow as someone who is willing to learn, for this time, the man no longer calls Jesus "Good Master." He just addresses him as "Master" or "Teacher." There is no effort to put Jesus on a pedestal.

When the man says he has followed these commandments since he was a youth, he is referring to that time when Jewish boys are initiated into adult responsibilities. Today this is called a *bar mitzvah*. It usually occurs when a boy is thirteen.

For Discussion: What does the man's answer tell us about his character?

TEXT TO READ: MARK 10:21

FIRST COMMENT ON THE TEXT: Mark's Gospel is dramatic and vivid—and full of emotion. Here Mark takes us inside Jesus' heart. He shows us Jesus looking at this man in a hurry, this man who has kneeled before him, this man who has done his best to keep the commandments. And Jesus, beholding him, loves him. Jesus' heart reaches out with compassion and grace. Many scholars believe the description here implies more than inner feeling. They think Mark is saying that Jesus physically reached out and embraced this man, hugged him, and held him close.

On one level, Jesus' words to the man are incredibly affirming and supportive. "You lack only one thing," Jesus tells him. "You've done well. You've been fair. You've been honest. You've killed no one. You've honored your father and mother. Never have you stolen. So there's only one thing more you need to do."

Wouldn't we all like to hear an unreserved affirmation like this from the lips of Jesus?

For Discussion: Why do you think Mark makes such a point of telling us that Jesus loved him? If you had been the man, and Jesus had embraced you, drawn you close, and whispered in your ear that there was only one thing that you lacked, how would you have been feeling?

SECOND COMMENT ON THE TEXT: The "one thing" that the man lacks is a right relationship with God's little ones. In this case, the little ones are not children or abused wives but "the poor." "Get up off your knees," Jesus tells the man, "and go and sell whatever you have. Go and sell whatever it is that makes you wealthy—whatever it is that makes you so full of yourself. Go and sell it—and then give to the poor."

Mark doesn't say exactly what the man is to give to the poor. All it says is "give to the poor." And perhaps, for Mark, the point of Jesus' command has nothing to do with a specific amount or even a specific percentage. Perhaps the point is to take away the man's status and privilege. Perhaps the point is to erase the boundaries and bridge the gap that keeps this man living for himself.

In Jesus' day, when an honored guest comes to your door, you not only welcome the guest into your home but also offer gifts—something to eat, something to drink, a comfortable place to sit. You might wash their feet or wipe their brow. That's how one would receive a guest.

Jesus is asking this man to receive the poor. He is asking him to receive God's little ones. He is asking him to receive those whom the world has cast aside. And in keeping with the customs of Jesus' day, he is asking him to receive by giving.

The man has asked what he must do to inherit eternal life. Jesus' answer is almost identical to what he told the disciples about the children they were sending away. When you receive the poor, when you give without hesitation and treat them like honored guests, then you are not just receiving the poor, says Jesus, for you are entering the kingdom of God. You are entering into life, eternal life, in the way that God intends. And thereby, says Jesus, you will have "treasure in heaven." Yes, says Jesus, when you break down the barriers, when you abandon your own sense of security, when you receive the poor and the weak, and when you give to those who have so little, you "inherit eternal life."

For Discussion: When you look at what Jesus says, how does it make you feel? To whom might he say the same today? In what ways do Jesus' words challenge both the fundamental spirit and structure of our world?

THIRD COMMENT ON THE TEXT: After telling the man to sell what he has and give to the poor, Jesus tells him to take up the cross that will surely be put in his path. In Jesus' day, the cross has only one meaning: it is a threat of death at the hands of the state. It is a tool of political control, a tool of political repression. Jesus has told his followers that they must take up any cross that's thrown in their way. They must not let it control them or intimidate them. They must not bow to the wrong authority.

By mentioning the cross in this context, Mark seems to understand that what Jesus has suggested here has tremendous political consequences. In effect Jesus' words undermine the class structure that keeps people apart. Jesus is threatening the status quo, in his day and ours, in a deep and fundamental way. He's abolishing the distinction between rich and poor, strong and weak, big and small. And those who hold power will fear such efforts.

In the mind of Jesus, there is but one community of believers. There is but one fellowship. There is but one body, marching together "to Zion, beautiful, beautiful Zion." As one body, "we join in a song with sweet accord." As one community of adults and children, men and women, rich and poor, educated and uneducated, people of diverse cultures and ethnic traditions, we "surround the throne." For as an old hymn says, it is all of us together, united in a way that abolishes all sense of status, who are "marching to Zion, the beautiful city of God."

Note: If you are breaking this session in half due to time constraints, this is the place to stop. When you resume, you can reestablish the context by first rereading the passage in Mark 10:13-21.

TEXT TO READ: MARK 10:22
BACKGROUND TEXT TO READ: MARK 4:19

COMMENT ON THE TEXT: The man who was in such a hurry, the man who was so eager, is now grieved. Mark never tells us what he does when he gets home. But Mark tells us he goes away deeply saddened, "for he had great possessions." Literally the text means that this man owns a lot of land. His property is vast. As a major landowner, he has a significant position in the community and among the leaders of the people. Because of that, he can feel superior to most of those around him. He can stick out his nose and look down on his neighbors. This man has wealth and status, but when it comes to treasure, he has little or none.

Jesus is asking this man who is in such a hurry to lift up the poor. He is asking him to unite his fortunes with theirs. He is asking him to think of the poor not as the least of his neighbors but as the greatest. Jesus is asking him to think of himself not as superior to those who have so little but as their brother. The man is to lift up rather than push down. He is to be "last of all, and servant of all." Thereby he will enter into treasure, for he will enter into that realm where God rules—and he will enter that realm not just as an observer but as a full and equal partner with all God's children.

But instead of entering into treasure, the man who has so eagerly run to Jesus now seems to slink away. As he fades away, our hearts tremble. Perhaps we remember a song by Margaret Douroux entitled, "Give Me a Clean Heart." Sometimes we, too, find ourselves pursuing riches and wealth. Sometimes we, too, want powerful people to know our name. But if breaking free is what we're after, then a clean heart is what makes that possible.

TEXT TO READ: MARK 10:23

COMMENT ON THE TEXT: This part of Mark is filled with references to Jesus' eyes. First we hear that Jesus beholds the man, who is in a great hurry. Somehow, the eyes of Jesus penetrate his soul. Jesus sees something within him that makes him love him. There is a sincerity, an honesty, a willingness to hear. Now, as the man goes off grieving, Jesus looks around again. Perhaps he is scanning the horizon for some sign of what the man will do. Perhaps he is looking at those who remain, those who have been willing to walk in his way.

Then Jesus turns to his disciples and shakes his head. "How hard it is," Jesus says, "for those who have riches to enter the kingdom of God." How hard it is for those with houses and lands to let God be God. How hard for those with wealth to see others as their equals, how hard for them to treat the poor as their sisters and brothers, how hard it is to break the spirit of arrogance, the spirit of exclusion!

For Discussion: The man whose grief provokes Jesus' comment is devout and religious. He believes in God, and he's been diligent in keeping certain of the commandments. So what is Jesus trying to say? What does it mean to enter the kingdom of God?

TEXT TO READ: MARK 10:24A

COMMENT ON THE TEXT: Mark tells us that the disciples are "astonished" at Jesus' words. They are shocked and amazed. He has already baffled them by saying that little children are as important as adults. He's baffled them by saying that women are as important as men. Now he is implying that the wealthy will find it hard to walk with God.

In Mark's day, many people see riches as a sign of God's blessing. It is an honor to be wealthy. The wealthy are at the top of society, and it is assumed that they are tops in God's eyes as well. Now Jesus is saying that it isn't so. The disciples can't believe it.

For Discussion: How are the rich viewed in our world? Do we ever wonder, as Jesus wondered, how the rich will ever enter the kingdom of God? Why is it that Jesus' words are still so astonishing and so puzzling to so many people?

TEXT TO READ: MARK 10:24B-25

COMMENT ON THE TEXT: Jesus sees his disciples' amazement. So he expands on his point. It's important for them to understand this truth. "Let me tell you how hard it is," Jesus says. "It's easier for a camel to squeeze through the eye of a sewing needle than for a person of wealth to enter the kingdom of God!"

Mark's Jesus has a wonderful sense of humor. So he chooses a colorful way of making his point. Camels are among the largest beasts that the people of Palestine ever see. Jesus asks his disciples to imagine one of these lumbering beasts squeezing through the tiny eye of someone's sewing needle. No way is it going to happen.

For Discussion: Why do you think it is so important to Jesus to make this point to his disciples? What Jesus says—do you think it's true? Why do so many who call themselves Christians find it hard to believe?

TEXT TO READ: MARK 10:26

For Discussion: Why do you think the disciples ask, "Who then can be saved?" What sort of attitude does this reflect? How does this attitude manifest itself in our own lives?

TEXT TO READ: MARK 10:27

FIRST COMMENT ON THE TEXT: Once again Mark mentions Jesus' eyes. Jesus has looked at the man in a hurry. He has looked around at the crowd. And now he looks at his disciples. He sees their bafflement. He sees the wrong spirit within them. And with his eyes, he penetrates their hearts. With his eyes, he bores through to the soul within them.

Then Jesus speaks. "Who can be saved?" he says. "Why do you even ask such a question? Do you think that it is by status or power or wealth that one gets into the kingdom of God? No, these are the ways of the world. The ways of God are not human but divine."

Perhaps at this point the disciples are despairing. Jesus seems to be saying that it's impossible to be saved. All the things that the world sees as important—they mean nothing to God. High people may know your name. You may be esteemed by friends and honored by family. Money may be falling out of your pockets. You may have more academic degrees than anyone can count. You may drive a high-class car and wear the finest dresses or suits. You may have jewelry that sparkles and shines. Politicians may stop by to chat. Bankers may bow when they see you approaching. But none of it will make a difference. For your entrance ticket to the kingdom of God has been declared invalid.

But then Jesus utters words of grace. What is impossible for us is possible for God. When we set aside our status, our power, our wealth, our false security, and our desire to be the greatest—when we have nothing left but Christ—then it's up to God and not us. And though it may seem that we have lost everything, we will have found the key to the door. For with God, all things are possible.

SECOND COMMENT ON THE TEXT: The Gospel of Mark seems to have been written for a struggling band of believers about thirty-five years after the killing of Jesus. And chances are, these believers are almost all desperately poor. The early band of believers for whom Mark writes would have no trouble singing that classic song by Kenneth Morris, "Christ Is All":

I don't possess houses or lands, fine clothes or jewelry.
Sorrows and cares in this old world my lot seems to be.
But I have a Christ who paid the price way back on Calvary.
And Christ is all, all in all, this world to me.

Perhaps Mark includes the story about the man in a hurry because he doesn't want the Christian community to expect much from the wealthy. He knows that more often than not, the rich, when they come running up, won't stay true. When push comes to shove, they will think first of themselves and their wealth. They will think of their land, their houses, their jewelry, their power and position too.

THIRD COMMENT ON THE TEXT: Now and then, a wealthier member of society might join the Christian band. Mark wants his readers to know that if such a miracle happens, it is all God's doing. With God, all things are possible. A rich convert is to be given no special honor, no special treatment. For it is God and God alone who makes a way out of no way.

The Hebrew Scriptures see wealth as a blessing from God. But Mark is here reminding us that the blessing is never meant for a single individual. Wealth is a blessing from God for the whole community. Jesus and Mark see individual wealth as a serious hindrance to the way of God. Wealth is given to be shared. Every member of the community is to be pulled up by it, whether they earn it or not, whether they deserve it or not. In the mind of Jesus, wealth is never earned, never deserved. Wealth is a blessing to be shared by all God's people.

For Discussion: If we as Christians heard Jesus' words, if we understood what he was saying, what would we do differently?

TEXT TO READ: MARK 10:28

For Discussion: What do you think Peter means by his statement?

TEXT TO READ: MARK 10:29-30

COMMENT ON THE TEXT: We don't know what Peter means by reminding Jesus about how the disciples have left jobs and homes and families to follow him. Mark doesn't tell us what the comment is all about. But it's a comment that many in the early church could have identified with. So the response of Jesus that Mark presents is an important one.

Jesus turns to Peter and says that, yes, there are many who have left their old houses. They have left brothers or sisters or fathers or mothers or wives or children. They have even given up lands for the sake of Jesus and the gospel. Then Jesus says that everyone who has done so will not be left alone. They may have given up their old world and their old ways. They may have given all they had to the poor. But every one of them shall receive—in the present time, in the present age—a multitude of blessings. They shall share houses and brothers and sisters. They shall find new mothers, new children, new lands.

Mark is not a false Gospel. It's brutally honest. So at the end of Jesus' list of blessings that will come in the present age there is an honest reminder: there will be persecutions as well. You don't upset the apple cart without arousing some wrath. You don't pursue a new vision and a new path without the heavy hand of the law coming down on you. You can't follow Jesus without stirring the fury of those who walk in Satan's ways. Mark doesn't mention persecution in the singular. It's plural: "persecutions."

But then, as soon as we are reminded of the persecutions that will befall us, we are also reminded of the promise of eternal life "in the world to come." In other words, no amount of persecution can defeat us. Even if we are killed, as Jesus will be, the way of evil has not triumphed. There is a "world to come." God is bringing it. And in that new world, there is "eternal life" for all who walk in God's new way.

For Discussion: In what ways might Jesus, if he were here today, expect us to leave houses or lands or families for the sake of the gospel? Mark says there will be blessings and persecutions for those who follow Jesus. Should Christians be more explicit in telling new believers to expect blessings as well as persecutions? Why do we so often forget to mention the persecution part of Mark's message?

TEXT TO READ: MARK 10:31

For Discussion: In what context have we heard these words in Mark before (Mark 9:35)? What does this repetition tell us about all the material that comes between these two verses that say essentially the same thing?

COMMENT ON THE TEXT: The Gospel of Mark is not just a random collection of stories and sayings. It's a carefully and deliberately crafted book. Its author has a passion for communication. And when we hear, for the second time, Jesus telling his disciples that "the first shall be last; and the last first," we know that the whole long section of Mark that comes between these sayings is all built around this same theme.

Jesus seems to have seen the need for a radical reversal. He envisions a time when those who have been pushed back will be brought forward. Those who have been ignored will be given places of honor. And those who have elevated themselves to the top of the social ladder will find themselves in a place that they don't expect. The powerful in our society have only a lukewarm regard (if that) for affirmative action plans. But God's affirmative action plan goes way beyond anything that the ruling class in the United States would ever accept. It's not just equality of opportunity for the future. It's a total and complete reversal.

In effect Jesus is addressing the world's little ones. He's talking to those children who have been thought of as worthless. He's talking to those wives who have been treated with contempt. He's talking with those who are poor and desperate, the hungry, the thirsty, the imprisoned. And he is telling them to "run on a little longer and see what the end will be."

At the same time, Jesus is telling his followers to unite themselves with those who are last now because those who are last now will be first in the world that is to come.

Dr. Martin Luther King Jr. said something similar, late in his life, when he told an assembled congregation not to despair, for there is "a creative force in this universe, working to pull down the gigantic mountains of evil." And this power is a God who makes a way out of no way, not just once but again and again.

WHEN STARS BEGIN TO FALL

MARK 13:14-32

Group leaders: This session, because of the interrelated and often misunderstood nature of its biblical texts, is longer than most. If you are using this material as a group Bible study and if your time is strictly limited, you may need to break this session in half, even though you will thereby lose an important sense of continuity. If you have to do that, a good place to stop is just before reading Mark 13:24a.

SETTING THE STAGE

PART ONE: In Mark's continuing drama, Jesus and the disciples are in Jerusalem, and they have just left the temple for the last time. As they go, the disciples express awe at the temple's grandeur. But Jesus tells them that it is a place of corruption that will be reduced to rubble. Not one stone will be left on another, he tells them. His words are a prophecy of judgment, a prediction of tumult and change.

The disciples are shocked, and they ask Jesus when these things will happen. In his answer, Jesus addresses the terrors and temptations that will come to his followers in the days that lie ahead. When Mark is written, a storm is about to break. Jewish rebels and Roman soldiers are fighting throughout Palestine. There are wars and rumors of wars, great famines resulting from the fighting, with violence on every hand. In the end, Jerusalem will be destroyed. The temple will be burned and defiled. By the year 70, the great Jerusalem temple, a showplace of the ancient world, will indeed be little more than a pile of rubble.

PART TWO: Mark 13 is the longest single section of direct teaching in the whole Gospel. Nowhere else does Mark go into such detail. But the emphasis is understandable. Mark seems to have been written in the midst of this war, and it's natural for him to spend more time than normal reminding his readers of those teachings that apply most directly to their immediate fears and concerns.

Mark 13 is structured around a series of reminders from Jesus to "watch" or "take heed." In the first section, Jesus tells his followers to take heed of others, lest someone lead them astray. Jesus is particularly concerned that his followers not be taken in by a sword-swinging political messiah. In the second section, Jesus tells his followers to take heed of themselves. They must not fall prey to adversity. They must not give in to fear. Don't worry about what to say, Mark reminds his readers. Even in the midst of a crisis, says Mark, hold to God's unchanging hand.

TEXT TO READ: MARK 13:14

FIRST COMMENT ON THE TEXT: Mark presents this verse, like others in the chapter, as a teaching of Jesus. It's part of the long answer that Jesus gives to James and John and Peter and Andrew after they come to him "in private" to learn more about what Jesus is talking about.

But the words of Mark are not always meant as a direct quotation of what Jesus said. Mark was not there, tape recording the words as they were spoken. What Mark gives us is his understanding of the underlying thrust of Jesus' message with as many of Jesus' distinctive phrases as he can muster.

But this verse shows us Mark interrupting the flow. The author of the Gospel breaks right in to wink at the reader and whisper, "Let the one who reads understand!" Mark is telling us that there is coded language in this verse. Jesus, in talking privately to the four disciples, might have been more direct. We don't know. What we do know is that the political situation in Mark's day is so extreme that Mark doesn't dare write the real meaning of this teaching. He has to resort to a code, which he pleads with his readers to understand.

For Discussion: As part of his code, Mark uses an image drawn from the Book of Daniel. Can you think of other situations in human history when people have had to use codes or hidden images to hide the real meaning of what they were saying? What is the purpose of codes? What does this tell us about the times in which Mark's first readers were living?

SECOND COMMENT ON THE TEXT: The code that Mark uses in this verse is a reference to the Book of Daniel. In some versions, it is translated as "the abomination of desolation." In others, it is "the desolating sacrilege" or "the awful horror." In Daniel, "the abomination of desolation" is the culmination of a time of great wickedness, a time when foreign powers and armies invade Jerusalem and do repulsive things in the midst of the temple of God. What they do in the temple is an abomination. In other words, it is so vile that it makes the temple desolate.

Some scholars believe that Daniel is talking about the horrors that happened in Jerusalem in 168 B.C.E. In that year, Greek armies led by the ruler Antiochus Epiphanes march into Jerusalem and set up a pagan altar in the temple, offering sacrifices to the god of war.

Although some Jews may have been seduced by the power and glory of this foreign ruler, his actions are enough to make most believing Jews gag and flee in horror. It is an abomination of the highest order for sacred places to be used in such a way. It would be something like the governor of Virginia deciding to carry out an execution in a church on a Sunday morning, right up front, while the congregation is celebrating holy Communion.

BACKGROUND TEXT TO READ: DANIEL 11: 31-35

For Discussion: What similarities do you notice between the scene described in Daniel 11 and the scene described in Mark 13? What are the similarities to our times?

THIRD COMMENT ON THE TEXT: Mark 13 is a reminder to the followers of Jesus to watch: "Beware! Look! Be alert! Keep awake!" When they see "the abomination" that makes desolate "standing where it ought not," then they are to flee. They are to run from Judea. They are to head to the mountains and not look back.

In the Greek text of Mark, the phrase that is normally translated "standing where it ought not" is literally "standing where he ought not." It's not usually translated that way because it doesn't make grammatical sense in English to switch from the impersonal "abomination" to the personal "he." But that's what Mark wrote.

Mark may mean that the abomination will come in the form of a person whose very presence will be an abomination. Or he may mean something bigger—that the abomination is the work of Satan. It may appear that it is others who are entering the temple, but perhaps in the mind of Mark and Jesus, it will be Satan who will be standing there. And that will be an abomination indeed.

FOURTH COMMENT ON THE TEXT: Scholars have tried to figure out what the reader is to understand from the coded reference to an abomination standing where "it [or, he] ought not."

Might it be a reference to the presence of armed rebels who use the temple as their headquarters and even carry out executions in its once-sacred halls? Might it be a reference to the Roman army that marches into the temple and plants a flag where no flag ought to be? Might it be a reference to the appointment of Phanni as the high priest during the winter of 67 and 68, an appointment that, according to historical records, causes at least one retired Jewish priest to weep and declare, "It would have been far better for me to have died before I had seen the house of God laden with such abominations"?

The Gospel of Mark is primarily a book about the good news of God's kingdom being close at hand. But you can't talk about God's work in the world without infringing on the world of politics and human powers. Mark knows, however, that he is on dangerous ground. If he speaks too plainly, the angry powers of evil will realize too clearly what he is saying. So he has coded his message. And that means that we will never fully know the specific events that he has in mind.

For Discussion: What kinds of insights should we gain from this verse for our day?

TEXT TO READ: MARK 13:14-16

FIRST COMMENT ON THE TEXT: These verses are filled with urgent political advice for those followers of Jesus who are living in Jerusalem in the midst of the bloody war between the Roman army and Jewish rebels. There is a crisis coming, Mark seems to be saying. When you hear of an abomination entering the temple, run—run for your lives. Fly—fly away.

Through repetition, Mark makes clear the teaching of Jesus. He makes clear that when the crisis hits, you have no time to linger. This is like those urgent calls that would go out to slaves who had a chance to ride the Underground Railroad to freedom. Mark is saying that when you hear the signal, you've got to move. If you're working on your housetop, as people often do, get to the ground as fast as you can. Don't go back into the house to gather up your possessions. Just fly—fly away.

In Jesus' day, people working outdoors often set their outer garment down beside the field. They don't need it while they are working. It is used to wrap up in at night to stay warm. So you set it down while you work. When the crisis comes, says Mark, don't go looking for your outer garment. Just fly—fly away.

SECOND COMMENT ON THE TEXT: Throughout Mark, Jesus talks to his followers about the importance of picking up certain things so that they can move forward in faith.

For example, a paralyzed man is told to take up his bed and walk. Those who are victims of political intimidation are told to pull up the crosses that are placed in their path, following in God's way anyhow. The disciples are told to gather up the few loaves and fishes that they have with them and then move out into the crowd and share their food with all who are hungry. In like manner, those who are victims of religious exclusion and oppression are told to pick up the mountain that's in their way and toss it into the sea. Mark's Jesus sets people free to walk on.

This passage has a similar theme. Toss aside whatever might hold you back, Jesus is saying. When the crisis comes, when the signal sounds, when the abomination stands where no abomination should ever stand, when the storms of life are raging more furiously than they have ever raged, just pick yourself up—and fly, fly away.

THIRD COMMENT ON THE TEXT: In this section of Mark, Jesus tells his followers to flee to the hills when the crisis comes. And there is historical evidence that this is what they did. According to some ancient records, just before the Roman destruction of Jerusalem and the burning and looting of the temple, most followers of Jesus suddenly abandoned the holy city.

According to these accounts, the followers of Jesus fled from the flames of war. They fled across the mountains to the town of Pella, on the far side of the Jordan River. Some thought they had been warned by an angel. Some thought they had seen a sign and remembered an old teaching of Jesus. Whatever the cause, the followers of Jesus knew the time had come. They headed out and didn't turn back.

Their flight was not merely an escape from the trials of war. It was also an act of resistance. It was a repudiation of the ways of violence. It was a repudiation of the ways of war. It was a repudiation of the ways of Satan. The town of Pella, where they fled, wasn't quite "down by the riverside," but it was close to it. And it's possible that it was there, in their own way, that the followers of Jesus first began to sing words later reflected in an old spiritual:

> Going to lay down my sword and shield, down by the riverside—
> Ain't gonna study war no more!

For another three centuries, long after the destruction of Jerusalem, the followers of Jesus are known throughout the Roman Empire as those who refuse to bow before any emperor or human ruler. They refuse to salute any flag, considering it idolatry. And they refuse, again and again, to serve in the military—no matter the cause, no matter the plea. They had learned that the ways of Satan are an abomination. They had learned that the ways of Satan make the house of God desolate, whether it is a building made of stone or a heart of flesh and blood. Whenever the ways of Satan came close, they knew it was time to fly—time to fly away.

For Discussion: What are the ways of Satan that Jesus might want us to flee from? What should be the attitude of Christians today toward flags and armies and mighty powers?

TEXT TO READ: MARK 13:17-19

COMMENT ON THE TEXT: Jesus says that the crisis that is coming will be a time of great "affliction." There will be sorrow and stress beyond belief. In the course of his instruction, he expresses great empathy for women and for all who have to endure such tragedies while caring for young children. They will suffer much. He sorrows as well for those who are forced to flee their homes in winter, for some will not make it.

TEXT TO READ: MARK 13:20

COMMENT ON THE TEXT: Jesus tells the disciples that the troubles that are coming are greater than any the world has ever known. They are the work of the Evil One. They are the fruit of Satan's labor. So there is no way that any human hand can lessen them. All human effort is in vain, for it is the Lord and the Lord alone who is able to shorten those days. It is the Lord and the Lord alone who can stand up to Satan and cause the pain to be lessened.

It is not that the pain will be eliminated. It is not that evil will disappear. It is only that it will be "shortened." We know not how evil this world would be if it were not for the compassionate hand of God. We know not how deep our suffering would be if it were not that God steps in, again and again, to lessen the pain, to shorten the suffering, to soften the blow.

God steps in, says Jesus, for the sake of the elect, which is to say, for the sake of those whom God has chosen, which is to say, for the sake of all those who hear God's voice and seek to walk in God's ways. The benefits of God's intervention are shared by all who endure affliction. But it is for the sake of those who honor God's reign that God steps in. For their sake, God shortens the pain for everyone.

The imagery here seems to be drawn in part from Daniel 12, where God intervenes in a great conflict on behalf of those whose names are written on the heavenly roll.

BACKGROUND TEXT TO READ: DANIEL 12:1

For Discussion: If God can step in to shorten the days and lessen the pain, why do you think God doesn't stop the evil in the first place?

TEXT TO READ: MARK 13:21-22

COMMENT ON THE TEXT: Jesus warns his followers not to be seduced by those who say they are new political messiahs. People will come trying to lure you into their violent political movements, says Jesus. They will tell you that by taking up the sword, you will free yourself from suffering and oppression. They will tell you that through force of arms, they will be able to bring your affliction to an end if only you will join them in their evil ways.

In Jewish thought, a true prophet could be seen through the doing of "signs and wonders." But Jesus tells his followers that signs and wonders aren't enough. These "false Christs" and "false prophets" will be able to do signs and wonders. They will appear to have power and glory. But if they don't walk in God's ways, then don't believe them, says Jesus. If they tell you that evil can be defeated through human strength, then don't believe them, says Jesus, for that is a task for God and God alone. And if they tell you that you can use a sword to banish the sword, or if they tell you that you can use an evil means to accomplish a good end, then don't believe them, for evil only begets evil.

The implication seems to be that if we are seduced by false messiahs, we will fail to fly away from the abominations of this world. Rather than breaking free, we will become entangled in the ways of Satan. We will become agents of the wrong king. And when the time comes to flee Jerusalem, when the time comes to fly away and not look back, we will fail to move. We will stay where we are. In the end, our pain will be greater, as will the suffering of our neighbor.

For Discussion: How are followers of Jesus seduced today?

TEXT TO READ: MARK 13:23

COMMENT ON THE TEXT: Here is the third command to "take heed" or to watch. The first command was to take heed lest others deceive us. The second command was to take heed lest we ourselves give in to fear or intimidation. This third command is to "take heed" about things that have been "foretold."

In other words, we are to watch what is happening around us. We are to watch the times. We are to be ready for any crisis, ready to move when any abomination comes close. By taking heed to the times, we will know when to flee. We will know when to fly away. We will know when to gather down by the riverside. We will know when to resist the forces of evil. We will know when to lay down our sword and shield and declare, with conviction, that we "ain't gonna study war no more."

But it is not just evil that we are to take heed of. We are also to watch for the hand of God, for Jesus has promised that God will lessen the pain and shorten the days. It may feel like we are enduring the deepest afflictions that have ever been or ever will be. Wars and famines and enslavements may rage around us. Women and children may cry in anguish. The harsh winds of winter may blow deep in our souls. We should recognize evil for what it is.

But we are to take heed to the good as well, for that too has been foretold. We are to watch for signs of God's intervention, signs of God's deliverance. As followers of Jesus, we are to have both open eyes and open hearts. We are to see the pain and feel the glory. We are to endure the sorrow and know the joy. In the midst of tribulation, when the storms of life are raging, we can still sing with Charles A. Tindley:

> *When the hosts of hell assail,*
> *and my strength begins to fail,*
> *Thou who never lost a battle, stand by me!*

Note: If you are breaking this session in half due to time constraints, this is the place to stop. When you resume, you can reestablish the context by first rereading Mark 13:14-23.

TEXT TO READ: MARK 13:24A

COMMENT ON THE TEXT: In the Jewish Scriptures, references to the "great day of the LORD" are often introduced with the words "in those days." When those words are used here, it's a clue that the next few verses will be about something bigger and grander than what has gone before.

For the first readers of Mark, "in those days" is a familiar phrase. It's a phrase that arouses feelings of hope, a sense of anticipation. Certain phrases, perhaps drawn from a song (like "Soon and very soon . . .") serve a similar function for us. But Mark wants to be sure that the hopeful feelings evoked here are not separated from reality. So immediately he reminds us that much suffering and tribulation will come first. His readers need to take heed of the big picture, but in the process they must not lose sight of immediate dangers. The great day of the Lord is coming, but it may not come until the midnight hour. Until then, we must watch those who would deceive us. And we must be ready to flee if the situation demands it.

"In those days," says Jesus, "the promised day of the LORD will dawn.

You can be sure of that. But don't go thinking that it will come before the suffering begins. Don't go thinking that you'll escape all trouble and tribulation. Evil is too strong. Evil is too real."

For Discussion: Why is it so important to keep in mind the reality of evil and the promise of God's future deliverance?

TEXT TO READ: MARK 13:24B-25

COMMENT ON THE TEXT: In these verses, we hear Jesus using cosmic imagery for that future day of the Lord, that time when God will turn the world on end and cause evil to be no more. Mark talks of the sun being darkened, the moon not giving its light, the stars of heaven falling, and the "powers" that are in heaven being shaken.

For Discussion: What kind of feelings do you think this imagery would foster in the hearts and minds of poor peasants in Palestine at the time this Gospel is written? What kinds of feelings does it evoke in us? What do you think it means when it says that "powers that are in heaven" will be shaken?

BACKGROUND TEXTS TO READ: ISAIAH 13:10-11; JOEL 3:15-16

COMMENT ON THE TEXT: These verses from Isaiah and Joel use images of the sun being darkened and the moon and the stars not shining as signs of the promised day that is yet to come when God will make all things new. The wickedness of tyrants will be brought to an end. The arrogance of the proud will be no more. The haughtiness of those who bring terror to others will be brought low. And then shall the Lord be the hope of all people, the strength of all who look to God for their salvation.

Both Jesus and the ancient Jewish prophets seem to understand the great power of evil. They see it as entrenched in the fabric of the universe. So when its grip on the world is finally shaken, it will be such a major event that the whole universe will rock and reel. The sun will go dark. The moon will fade away. Stars will shine no more. The universe will tremble, for the roots of hate and violence run deep. They are not easily moved aside. When God triumphs over evil, the whole universe will feel it.

To many of the Jewish prophets and to Jesus, the powers of evil are like the stars. They rise way above the level of human existence. They are greater than anything we can imagine. Perhaps that is why, in Jewish thought, the powers of evil are thought to reside in the heavens.

Yet in the mind of the Jewish prophets and in the mind of Jesus, God is greater. God is stronger. That's why it says in Mark 13:24-25 that the "stars" will fall and the "powers" that reside in the heavens will be shaken. It's not the power of God that will be shaken. It is the entrenched power of evil that will come crashing down.

For Discussion: What do you think of the way that the Gospel of Mark portrays the power of evil? Is it that big? The Gospel says that though evil is big, its fall is sure. What do you think that means for how we should live?

TEXT TO READ: MARK 13:24-26

COMMENT ON THE TEXT: According to the Gospel of Mark, it is only after the universe is shaken, the sun is darkened, and the stars begin to fall that the world will see the Son of Man, which is Jesus, coming with power and glory.

The world doesn't much notice the first time he comes. The powers of his day seem blind to his power and his glory. But when the universe is shaken, when evil is defeated, then the veil will be lifted, says Mark. The world will finally see Jesus for who he is.

Then they who have fallen by the wayside, then they who have wandered from the path of love, then they who have sold their souls to the perverted ways of death will be sorrowful indeed, for they will see and know the truth. Among those who practice evil, laughter will turn to weeping. And scoffing will turn to mourning. The words of an old spiritual express it well:

My Lord, what a mourning, when the stars begin to fall!

BACKGROUND TEXT TO READ: DANIEL 7:9-13

COMMENT ON THE TEXT: Much of the imagery in this part of Mark is designed to evoke the words of the Jewish prophets, and the reference to the Son of Man coming on the clouds to receive power and glory is no exception. The Jewish Scriptures include many references to God coming "in the clouds" or "with the clouds." But the most direct parallel to Jesus' words can be found in Daniel 7, where one like a "son of man" comes on the clouds to destroy the power of those "beasts" who perpetuate the ways of evil. These are perhaps the same beasts that are referred to early in the Gospel, when Jesus faces down Satan in the wilderness.

BACKGROUND TEXT TO READ: MARK 1:13

COMMENT ON THE TEXT: The Jesus whom we meet in this Gospel is truly the mighty One. From the beginning, he is able to resist the temptation to join forces with Satan and the "wild beasts." Instead of giving in to the ways of evil, again and again he sets free those whom the forces of evil have bound. And according to Mark 13, one day, when the heavens are shaken and evil stars go falling, this same child of Adam will come on the clouds, as it were. He will come to accept the honor and glory that is due his name.

For Discussion: What practical difference should this make for us?

TEXT TO READ: MARK 13:27

FIRST COMMENT ON THE TEXT: For those who know Jesus merely as a humble healer or as a worshipful Jew, this verse contains several startling statements.

Jesus tells the disciples that when the heavens are shaken and the stars go falling, he will send his angels to the far corners of the universe. Notice the pronoun: the angels are "his." They hear his voice. They answer his call. Like all of us, he may be a son of man. Like all of us, he may be an offspring of Adam. But there is more to Jesus than meets the eye.

And those angels who hear his cry will gather not just anyone. They will gather his elect. Those who walk in God's ways belong to him. They are his—and he is theirs. Without fear of error, they can truly sing, in the words of a hymn by Fanny Crosby:

> *I am thine, O Lord, I have heard thy voice,*
> *And it told thy love to me;*
> *But I long to rise in the arms of faith,*
> *And be closer drawn to thee.*

SECOND COMMENT ON THE TEXT: Equally startling, in a way, is the declaration that these angels whom Jesus sends out will gather God's elect from "the uttermost part of the earth." In a time of competing national allegiances—at a time when Roman armies battle Jewish rebels, at a time when nation is rising against nation—Jesus declares that those who have chosen God will come from "the uttermost part of the earth."

There are no national boundaries with God. There are no national allegiances. The people of God don't salute a particular flag. They don't pledge a particular allegiance. They don't belong to Rome. Nor do they belong to the powers that are struggling for control in Jerusalem. They find their identity in Jesus. They are his and his alone.

The affirmation that angels will search the uttermost parts of the earth and even the uttermost parts of heaven is also a word of comfort to those who are refugees. It is a word of inclusion for all who are forced to flee from danger, to run for their lives, or to hide in secret places to survive, as so many have had to do over the centuries.

Yes, says Jesus, you may have to flee from the beasts. Evil may get so strong that you have to drop everything and run for the hills. But when you flee, know this: God's angels will find you. When the heavens have been shaken, when the stars begin to fall, God's angels will gather you up. They will bring you back. There will be a great assembly of the faithful, a great congregation of the redeemed.

TEXT TO READ: MARK 13:28-29

FIRST COMMENT ON THE TEXT: Jesus now asks his followers to "learn" a parable. Not to memorize it but to understand its meaning in a deep and life-changing way.

Think about the fig tree, says Jesus. When its branch is tender, when the sap is flowing and it begins to put out leaves, you know that summer is near. The leaves are a sign of what will follow. In the same way, says Jesus, when you see horrible things come to pass—when you see the temple burned and defiled, when you see armies marching against armies, when you have to flee to the hills for safety—remember that these things are only a prelude to what will follow. Remember that the day of the Lord is nigh. The day when the heavens will shake. A day when stars will fall. A day when tyrants will be no more.

SECOND COMMENT ON THE TEXT: The command to watch or take heed isn't literally found in this section. Nevertheless Jesus tells his followers to see through the horrors around them, to see through to the summer that lies ahead.

Just as the leaves you see on the fig tree are a sign that summer is coming, says Jesus, so too the sufferings of this world are a sign that beasts will not always triumph. Armies will not always march. Hate will not always endure. When we see through the horrors around us, we will see the Son of Man, the Mighty One, coming on the clouds. Then the days of evil will be over. Then, from every corner of this world, the faithful will be gathered. Then, from every secret hiding place, those who endure will give honor and glory to that one whose deeds are love.

For Discussion: What kinds of horrors do we need to see through?

TEXT TO READ: MARK 13:30

COMMENT ON THE TEXT: Mark begins to wrap up an important loose end in this conversation. This long series of teachings from Jesus begins with four of the disciples coming to Jesus privately, after Jesus has foretold the destruction of the temple. In Mark 13:4, they ask him, "When shall these things be? And what shall be the sign when all these things shall be fulfilled?" And Jesus hasn't answered their question.

Now, however, Jesus turns to the disciples, "Verily, the tumbling of the temple is not in some far-off time, for these things which you asked me about so privately, they will come to pass before the current generation is gone. Many who are living today will see them happen."

The four disciples have asked when these things will happen. They have also asked for a sign of when they are about to occur. But with his parable of the fig tree, Jesus has turned the disciples' request on its head. Instead of giving them a sign of when the troubles in Jerusalem will begin, he tells them that the troubles themselves will be a sign—a sign of the summer that is near, a sign that the heavens will be shaken, a sign that the power of evil will be broken, a sign that stars will fall and hate will die. Their generation will see, says Jesus. Their generation will know the truth, if they will but see through the horrors around them.

TEXT TO READ: MARK 13:31

BACKGROUND TEXT TO READ: PSALM 102:25-27

COMMENT ON THE TEXT: Immediately after telling his disciples that great crises are coming, even in their own generation, Jesus reminds them that through it all, God remains. Jesus' words seem designed to bring to mind the words of Psalm 102. Mark may be trying to show us Jesus paraphrasing the psalm for his disciples. Like the psalm, Jesus says that heaven and earth may pass away, but God's word—the word of truth and hope and love, the very seed that Jesus has been planting—that word will forever endure.

TEXT TO READ: MARK 13:32

COMMENT ON THE TEXT: Jesus seems to understand the question that will arise for his followers. If the sorrow and suffering that comes with the destruction of Jerusalem is a sign that summer is surely coming, if it's a sign that the heavens will be shaken and all evil powers knocked from their thrones, then when will this cosmic revolution occur? When will the old order come to an end? When will we see the dawning of God's new world?

Don't be fooled, says the Gospel of Mark. To questions such as these, there is no answer. No human anywhere knows the day or the hour that evil will be no more. Don't let anyone tell you otherwise, for neither the angels nor Jesus knows when it is that God will bring the forces of hate crashing down. It is enough, says Jesus, to know that summer is coming. It is enough, says Jesus, to know that violence will not forever endure. It is enough, says Jesus, to know that God's promise is sure.

Mark seems to believe that when we live in the promise, when we see through the horrors, we will still have much evil to deal with. We will still have much sorrow to endure. But when we live in the promise, when we see through the horrors, the grip of evil will be broken.

Chains may still bind us on the outside, but on the inside we will be breaking free. We will be running forward in hope, looking to that day when the Son of Man will come riding on the clouds, that day when the sun will be darkened, that day when all God's people will be gathered, that day when, amid great singing and shouting, the stars begin to fall.

SESSION 15

AND IMMEDIATELY,
WHILE HE YET SPAKE,
COMETH JUDAS,
ONE OF THE TWELVE,
AND WITH HIM A
GREAT MULTITUDE
WITH SWORDS
AND STAVES. . .
—MARK 14:43

WHEN YOUR ENEMIES ASSAIL

MARK 14:32-52

Group leaders: This session is longer than some. If you are using this material as a group Bible study and if your time is strictly limited, you may need to break this final session in half, even though you will thereby lose some dramatic continuity. If you have to do that, a good place to stop is just before reading Mark 14:43.

SETTING THE STAGE

PART ONE: In Mark's powerful drama, Jesus and the disciples celebrate Passover in a secret room. During the meal, Jesus passes the bread of affliction—the unleavened bread—and describes it as his body, which will be battered and broken. But he says that, like the bread of affliction, it will become the bread of freedom.

Then he passes the Passover cup to the very people who will betray him and deny him. He calls the cup "my blood of the covenant," thereby connecting himself both to the old blood of the covenant mentioned in Exodus and to the future blood of the covenant mentioned by the prophets Ezekiel, Jeremiah, and Zechariah. Through his words, he reminds them that God's promised Savior is coming, humble and riding on an ass.

This promised Savior, according to the prophets, will not be the ruler of a single nation or an exclusive people. Rather, this king will reign from sea to sea, over all the earth. He will break the battle bow and speak peace rather than war. No more violence for him.

PART TWO: Next Mark shows his readers Jesus telling the disciples that this promised kingdom is so close that the next time he drinks wine with them, it will be in that new kingdom. Then Jesus and the disciples sing a hymn, probably Psalm 118, which is traditionally sung at the end of a Passover celebration. The psalm reminds its hearers that God's mercy endures forever for all people. It also reminds its hearers that the stone that human builders reject will someday become the chief cornerstone in the new temple that God is building, a house not made with hands.

Mark then makes a point of telling his readers that Jesus and the disciples go to the Mount of Olives, which the prophets have described as a place from which God's deliverance will come. And, as they go, Jesus declares to his disciples that on this night every one of them will be scandalized and offended by him. Their disgust will reveal the truth about their hearts. Their disgust will show who they serve.

But don't worry, says Jesus. This is the scattering of the sheep that the prophets foretold. And the scattering of sheep will ultimately be a good thing, like a refiner's fire.

PART THREE: By mentioning the scattering of the sheep, Mark brings to mind for us, his readers, the words of those prophets who talk about this. He is reminding us that the scattering will be followed by God gathering together the scattered sheep and establishing for them a covenant of peace. The evil beasts will be banished. The big bully will be bound. And in place of violence will come showers of blessing for all people. No one will need to be afraid any more.

None of the disciples seem to understand. Peter interrupts and claims that he will never be scandalized or offended by Jesus. But in denying

Jesus' statement, in declaring Jesus wrong, Peter has already shown his ability to turn against his teacher.

Mark lets us imagine Jesus shaking his head in amazement. Then Jesus returns to a note of hope. Using more language from the Passover, Jesus tells the disciples that just as God went before the people of Israel as they left Egypt, to guide their way, so too, after he is risen, he will "go before" them and show them the way—a way that they have so far found hard to accept.

TEXT TO READ: MARK 14:32

COMMENT ON THE TEXT: Gethsemane seems to be one of the many olive orchards that are found in Jesus' day near the base of the Mount of Olives. In Hebrew, its name means "Place of the Oil Press." In Jesus' day, many olive orchards have their own press to make oil.

It's late, perhaps after midnight. And here in the shadows of the orchard, among the scraggly olive trees, Jesus tells the disciples to sit and wait while he goes off to pray.

There are only three times in the whole Gospel that Mark tells us that Jesus prays. And each time Jesus prays, he seems to be exhausted. He prays alone. He prays at night. And in Mark's drama, each time, it is in the midst of Jesus' deep awareness of how close and how strong the power of the demonic is. He prays as a way of reaching out to God so that he might overcome the power and lure of Satan.

For Discussion: What should we learn from the pattern of prayer that Mark presents in his Gospel? How well does this pattern of prayer fit or not fit with what you have seen or experienced?

TEXT TO READ: MARK 14:33

For Discussion: Jesus has said that all twelve of the disciples will be scandalized and offended by him. So why do you think Mark shows us Jesus taking these three with him while he prays?

FIRST COMMENT ON THE TEXT: With his careful sensitivity to good literary technique, Mark never explains why Jesus drags these three disciples with him through the olive trees to a praying place in the orchard at Gethsemane. But in the revealing light of the larger picture painted in the Gospel, Mark thinks we will understand.

Mark thinks we will remember James and John proudly asking for exclusive seats of power next to Jesus when Jesus comes into his glory. Through their question, they show that they are thinking of him as a political messiah who will need people to help him rule the nation of Israel. They want to be with him at the top. Jesus questions whether they are ready to drink the cup that he will drink. And they say they're ready.

In like manner, Mark probably thinks we will remember Peter, who moments before has contradicted Jesus and claimed that he is going to be with him all the way, no matter what. These three boasters are about to confront the truth about themselves. By allowing us to see their failings, Mark perhaps wants us to recognize our own failings as well.

SECOND COMMENT ON THE TEXT: Throughout the Gospel, Mark only rarely hints at Jesus' inner feelings. This verse is an exception. The feelings that it describes are deep and profound.

The King James Version says that Jesus "began to be sore amazed, and to be very heavy." Other translations do a better job of conveying the intensity of what is described, for the Greek words used by Mark imply a great distress and a profound inner agitation. It is as if Jesus is literally shuddering and staggering under the weight of his anguish. He is deeply disturbed. He is perhaps panting and short of breath. He is tossed and driven. There's a trembling in his soul.

For Discussion: What causes us to have similar feelings?

TEXT TO READ: MARK 14:34

COMMENT ON THE TEXT: Jesus is in distress. Sweat pours from his brow. His body trembles. Anguish pours from the depth of his soul, for the cosmic forces of the universe are in deep conflict. Satan is raging like a roaring lion. The strong man is baring his teeth, preparing to pounce. The bully of the universe is about to gather more victims.

Jesus, struggling to be true to God, struggling not to abandon God's ways, is staggering under the weight of it all. The universe is moving toward a crisis—and Jesus is caught in it.

The language of this verse brings to mind for Mark's readers the words of Psalm 42. Mark seems to be suggesting that this psalm's combination of despair and hope reflects the inner turmoil that Jesus is feeling.

BACKGROUND TEXT TO READ: PSALM 42

For Discussion: Is it possible to feel hope and despair at the same time? What kinds of situations might arouse such a combination of feelings?

TEXT TO READ: MARK 14:35

COMMENT ON THE TEXT: In Jesus' day, it is common to fall on the ground while praying, especially when feeling distress. It is a position of humility. From this position, in Jesus' day, people pray aloud, for silent prayer and even silent reading are unknown concepts.

In the scene as Mark describes it, Jesus prays that "the hour" might pass from him. He means this in a figurative sense, for it isn't just a period of sixty minutes that is troubling Jesus. It is the whole period of time that lies ahead. He pleads with God to be excused from what is about to unfold. He feels overwhelmed with the awfulness of it all. He wants out if he possibly can.

For Discussion: What do you think Mark is trying to tell us about Jesus' impending execution? How do you think Mark wants us to see Jesus—as a powerful hero, "marching as to war," knowing victory is his, or as a trembling victim of evil forces that are rising up against God and God's ways? Why do you think Mark is making such a distinction? How might this be connected to what the disciples are scandalized about?

TEXT TO READ: MARK 14:36

COMMENT ON THE TEXT: Now and then, Mark includes in his Gospel some words in Aramaic, which is a language related to Hebrew. It's the language that natives of Galilee probably speak most often in Jesus' day. In Aramaic, *Abba* means "my father." It has a familiar, affectionate feel. It's a term one would use at home, not in public. Seldom, if ever, is it a name used for God.

Earlier in the Gospel, we see Jesus calling those who do the will of God his sisters, his brothers, his mother. Now, in this trembling prayer, we see him addressing God not as a distant Lord but as a much-loved member of his own household. "Abba, Father!" he says.

"With you, everything is possible," says Jesus. "So I ask you—I plead with you—take this cup away from me! Please, make some other way!" Jesus does not seek to impose his desires. He does not threaten or demand. He only pleads. He puts God's will first, not his own.

In Jesus' day, one's prayers might include excerpts from a psalm that expresses feelings or emotions similar to one's own. Many people could recite psalms from memory. In this case, the plea that Mark puts on Jesus' lips matches the feel of the plea in Psalm 140. And it's possible that Mark means for us to think of that psalm as part of Jesus' prayer.

BACKGROUND TEXT TO READ: PSALM 140:1-8

For Discussion: How does the imagery of this psalm fit or not fit with the theological images of Jesus that Mark has been painting in the last few verses? Do you think that we, through our words and songs, accurately convey this image of Jesus? Or are we, like the disciples, a little offended by it and thus create a picture that is more triumphant?

BACKGROUND TEXTS TO READ: PSALM 60:3; ISAIAH 51:17-23

FIRST COMMENT ON THE TEXT: When Mark shows us Jesus staggering under the weight of the anguish in his soul, pleading with God that the cup be taken from him, it's likely that Mark is directing our thoughts to some other texts as well, for several passages in the Jewish Scriptures talk about a cup that causes one to stagger and reel.

A few verses back in Mark, Jesus talks about sheep that have lost their shepherd and are scattered. In Psalm 60 and in Isaiah 51 we read about the city of Jerusalem reeling from wine that has made it drunk. This is not the wine of liberation but the wine of devastation. Isaiah says that there has been "none to guide her." The shepherds are sleeping. The children have passed out. They lie in a stupor on every street.

But to this drunken city—to this city without a shepherd—the Sovereign of the universe, the great King of all the earth, the Good Shepherd says this: "Stand up! I will be with you! And I will take from your hand the cup of staggering."

It seems likely that when Mark shows us Jesus staggering unto the weight of his anguish, pleading with God to take this cup from him, Mark wants us to think of Isaiah, where God indeed promises to take the cup of staggering from the people of Jerusalem.

Throughout his ministry, Jesus has encouraged others to take up their bed and walk. He has given courage in the face of adversity. Now he himself is beaten down. He trembles within, and as he lies prone on the ground, crying to God to take this cup from him, Mark points us to Isaiah, where God calls on those who are staggering to stand up, knowing that in time the cup of staggering will be taken from them.

SECOND COMMENT ON THE TEXT: In effect Mark is showing us Jesus struggling to walk in God's way. He shows us Jesus, fallen to the ground, overwhelmed with the evil that is rising up around him. He shows us Jesus, fallen to the ground, not sure he can stand. He shows us Jesus, fallen to the ground, struggling to find the courage and the strength to go on.

Like those described in Isaiah, his body feels like the bread of affliction, the unleavened bread that he passed to the disciples. He is being stepped on and walked on. In the face of such devastation, in the face of such staggering, in the face of such monumental evil, it's not easy to stand. It's not easy to follow. It's not easy to walk in God's way.

And yet, in the silence of this night, amid the shadows of the olive orchard, as his heart shudders within him, Jesus hears the voice of "Abba, Father" calling to him. Calling him to stand. Calling him to follow. Calling him to believe that though the cup of staggering seems heavy, it will not last forever. It will be lifted by God's hand—if only Jesus will stand, if only Jesus will follow.

The faith that Jesus struggles to find is the faith expressed by an old hymn, the faith to act before a way has been made, the faith to follow even when the burdens are heavier than you think you can bear. It's the faith that was affirmed by Charles A. Tindley, a man born to slave parents who became the pastor of a large Methodist church in Philadelphia, a church that originally had hired him only as its janitor:

> *When your enemies assail, and your heart begins to fail,*
> *Don't forget that God in heaven answers prayer.*
> *He will make a way for you, and will lead you safely through.*
> *Take your burden to the Lord—and leave it there!*

For Discussion: What kinds of burdens weigh down people in our world? In what kinds of situations have you seen people stand, even before a cup of staggering has been lifted?

TEXT TO READ: MARK 14:37

COMMENT ON THE TEXT: In Mark's drama, Jesus comes back to where he left Peter, James, and John. They're asleep. They know his pain. Yet they sleep.

Jesus shakes Peter awake, the one who so recently declared his loyalty.

And instead of addressing him as Peter, using the nickname Jesus gives him early in the Gospel, Jesus addresses him as "Simon," the only time in Mark's Gospel that we will hear Jesus address Peter this way. "Simon," says Jesus, "have you gone to sleep on me? Couldn't you be faithful for one hour?"

For Discussion: Do you think Jesus' comments are meant as a friendly jest—or a bitter jibe? Why? Why do you think Mark shows us Jesus now addressing Peter as Simon?

TEXT TO READ: MARK 14:38

For Discussion: What are the disciples supposed to watch for? What are they supposed to pray about? What is the "temptation" that they might enter into? What form might that temptation take in our world?

TEXT TO READ: MARK 14:39-40

For Discussion: What do you think Mark is trying to communicate by describing how often Jesus comes back to find the disciples sleeping?

TEXT TO READ: MARK 14:41

FIRST COMMENT ON THE TEXT: Scholars are unsure whether Jesus' words in this verse are meant as an observation or a biting question. Because old Greek manuscripts contain no punctuation marks, the words can be interpreted either way. Perhaps Jesus merely sighs and observes what is happening: "You still sleep. You still rest." Or perhaps Jesus is asking the biting question, "Are you still asleep? Are your eyes still closed? Are you still off in another world?"

Whichever it might be, the feeling is akin to an old Negro spiritual:

O, way down yonder, by myself—and I couldn't hear nobody pray!

In like manner, the words translated in some versions as "it is enough" are probably not meant as a statement by Jesus about the adequacy of the effort put forth by his disciples. In fact, the Greek word that is translated as "enough" has strong commercial connotations. It's used in Jesus' day to mean that a bill has been paid or that a commercial transaction is complete because enough has been paid.

SECOND COMMENT ON THE TEXT: So it's possible that what Mark wants us to understand is that the time for watching and praying is over. Money has changed hands. Frightened "shepherds" have turned coins over to Judas, coins bearing the image of the Roman caesar.

Perhaps Mark is presenting us with a Jesus who has been bought and sold, a Jesus who cleansed the temple of its sacrifice sellers and money changers but who has now become one of their victims, bought and sold like a dove or goat—or Passover lamb.

Perhaps Mark is telling us that the Son of Man, this offspring of Adam who is so much like ourselves, has been betrayed into the hands of sinners, into the hands of those who do Satan's will, who follow Satan's ways, who are themselves victims of the strong man.

THIRD COMMENT ON THE TEXT: The cup of staggering is heavy upon Jesus. But Jesus stands. And Jesus follows in God's way. He sets fear aside, for he knows that God's kingdom is close, the covenant of peace, the reign that knows no end.

Violence is rising. Demonic powers are ready to make Jesus their next victim. But the "Abba, Father" to whom Jesus prays has promised to break the bow of battle and banish evil beasts from the earth. Jesus is watching. Jesus is praying. Though he staggers, yet he stands.

Will we be sleepers, Mark seems to be asking, or watchers? Will we recognize the power of the demonic when it comes close—or will we shut our eyes and take our rest? When the cup of staggering is passed to our lips, will we find the courage to stand—or will we collapse in exhaustion and plant on our hearts the image of Caesar rather than the image of God? Will we bow to the oppressor—or to the Savior?

The scene in Gethsemane gives us deep insight into Jesus. But Mark means for it to give deep insight into ourselves as well. He believes we will all be beaten. We will all be battered. We will all be stomped upon. He wonders, when evil rises up, if we will fall away or if we will sing, with eyes open, the contemporary gospel song entitled "Lord, Help Me to Hold Out!"

TEXT TO READ: MARK 14:42

COMMENT ON THE TEXT: The shuddering and staggering Jesus, who has described his soul as "exceeding sorrowful," must rouse his sleeping disciples, who have been no support to him. The one who is so weighed down must now be the one to tell his disciples to "rise up." We must be going, he tells them, for the traitor is fast approaching.

For Discussion: How can we avoid being like the disciples in our relationships with others?

Note: If you are breaking this session in half due to time constraints, this is the place to stop. When you resume, you can reestablish the context by first rereading Mark 14:32-42.

TEXT TO READ: MARK 14:43

COMMENT ON THE TEXT: Mark makes this scene very dramatic. It is presumably after midnight. There is always a full moon at Passover, and Jesus and the disciples are deep in the shadows of an olive orchard, near the Mount of Olives. The tension is high. Suddenly, while Jesus and the disciples are talking, Judas appears. Judas—one of their own, one of the Twelve whom Jesus chose to be with him.

But now Judas comes not with Jesus but with the opposite of Jesus. He comes with an armed band of enforcers sent out by the chief priests and by the wealthy landowners, known as elders, and by the scribes, many of whom are Pharisees. The priests and elders and scribes don't come themselves. They send armed thugs. These agents are employed by the Sanhedrin, which is the ruling council of Jerusalem. These armed men function as the city's police officers. According to historical records, they often use swords and heavy clubs to break up any political protests or demonstrations that get too close to the temple.

TEXT TO READ: MARK 14:44

COMMENT ON THE TEXT: The police aren't sure that they will recognize Jesus in the darkness of this Passover night. So the armed thugs are told to arrest whomever Judas kisses.

At this time, a kiss is the normal greeting between disciples and their rabbi. It is common for a student to greet a teacher with a kiss. It's a sign of affection and friendship, an indication of loyalty and oneness, a token of honor and respect.

We're never told why Judas becomes a traitor, but Mark portrays the initial decision as coming just after Jesus has dinner in the home of a leper and just after Jesus praises the love and generosity of an unnamed woman who anoints his head with a fragrant and expensive oil (Mark 14:3-11). It is as if Jesus has once again turned over the social order, accepting the gracious gift of a woman rather than arming his male disciples for an armed assault on Jerusalem. Maybe Jesus isn't the kind of messiah that Judas had in mind. And maybe, in that sense, Judas has merely seen the truth about Jesus more quickly than the others.

In the King James Version, Judas tells the officers to lead Jesus away "safely." But it is the officers' safety, not Jesus' safety, that Judas is concerned about. He's telling them to hold Jesus tight. Keep him under guard. Don't let him get away—or this mission won't be a success.

For Discussion: What do you think is going on in the minds of those people who are sent out with Judas to arrest Jesus? How is their situation like or unlike situations we might find ourselves in? Are there times that we too find ourselves functioning as agents of evil and don't know how to escape? When that happens, what can we do?

TEXT TO READ: MARK 14:45

COMMENT ON THE TEXT: Judas wastes no time. He goes straight to Jesus, addresses him as "Master" or "Rabbi," and then kisses him. The sign of respect has become the token of contempt. The sign of loyalty has become the token of disgust. The sign of enduring friendship has become the token of violent betrayal.

TEXT TO READ: MARK 14:46

COMMENT ON THE TEXT: Mark loves irony. It's part of what gives his Gospel such penetrating power. So here he describes the armed thugs as laying their hands on Jesus. Those who carry swords and clubs and walk in the way of violence and intimidation lay hands on the one who has continually laid his hands on others: to heal, to affirm, to encourage, to feed, to bless.

In Mark's eyes, the contrast couldn't be more stark. He wonders which way we will walk and whose way we will follow. Will we lay hands on others to heal and affirm? Or will we walk with those who lay hands on others to harm and destroy?

TEXT TO READ: MARK 14:47

FIRST COMMENT ON THE TEXT: Throughout the Gospel, Mark demonstrates a sense of humor. He includes certain details because of their comic effect. This may be one of those scenes.

Without explanation, Mark tells us that someone yanks out a sword, and as the sword is flung about, off comes the ear of one of the servants of the high priest. To us, it sounds like something out of a slapstick comedy movie.

In one of the other Gospels, there's a reference to Peter cutting off a part of someone's ear and Jesus healing it. But there's none of that here. Instead, the few details that we read almost function like comic relief. From the scene as Mark describes it, it's only the armed thugs who carry swords. And historically, it's not likely that common people would have a sword at their side, especially when they've gone to an orchard to pray.

So it seems as if Mark wants us to see one of the officers comically pulling out a sword, and in his clumsiness, he chops off the ear of the high priest's servant, who has come along to make sure everything goes according to script.

SECOND COMMENT ON THE TEXT: Another function of this comic interlude might be to remind us of the earlier statement in Mark 4, where Jesus pleads for hearing on the part of all who have ears to hear—lest whatever hearing we have be taken from us.

The temple establishment, as represented in this scene by the high priest's servant, seems to have closed itself off from the good news that Jesus has proclaimed. And now, here in Gethsemane, by resorting to violence and the forceful ways of the big bully, the temple establishment is, as we might put it, shooting itself in the foot. Or, as Mark might put it, the temple establishment is cutting off its own ear.

BACKGROUND TEXT TO READ: MARK 4:23-25

For Discussion: In what ways might we sometimes cut off our ears? Are there actions that cause us to lose our understanding of the good news that Jesus proclaimed?

COMMENT ON THE TEXT: The attitude that Mark seems to want his readers to have is the attitude expressed in the second verse of an old hymn by Clara Scott, where she writes:

Open my ears, that I may hear
Voices of truth thou sendest clear;
And while the wave notes fall on my ear,
Ev'rything false will disappear.
Silently now, I wait for thee,
Ready, my God, thy will to see;
Open my ears,
Illumine me, Spirit divine!

TEXT TO READ: MARK 14:48

For Discussion: What does the use of swords and clubs say about how well the temple authorities have understood Jesus' message? Why do you think they misunderstand so badly?

COMMENT ON THE TEXT: For Mark, the words in Mark 14:48 are filled with sadness and irony. Jesus turns to the thugs that the priests and scribes and elders have sent. Do you think of me as a "thief," as someone you must come against with weapons, he asks.

The word that Mark uses here for "robber" or "thief" is the same distinctive Greek word that he uses in Mark 11, where Jesus overthrows the tables in the temple and accuses the temple leadership of turning the house of God into a "den of thieves" (Mark 11:17). The Greek word describes someone who ruthlessly exploits others, not just someone who steals but someone who steals through use of violence and force. Is this who you think I am, Jesus asks. Is the world of robbery and violence the only world you know?

In Jesus' day, political revolutionaries are also called robbers. That's because they too use violence. It is common, when Mark is written, for armed guerrillas to stop people by force on rural roads and forcibly take what they have in order to finance the revolution and provide needed food for those who are pursuing violent revolt.

Such a model has nothing to do with what Jesus has taught or with what Jesus has done. Yet that's how the governing authorities see him.

TEXT TO READ: MARK 14:49-50

FIRST COMMENT ON THE TEXT: "You have had many chances to arrest me," says Jesus. "Was I not in the temple daily?" By reminding the temple police of this, Jesus is reminding them of their weakness. The temple authorities have been afraid of Rome and how Rome might react if something isn't done about Jesus. Yet they've also been afraid to arrest him. They've been afraid to do anything that might cause a stir. They pretend to have power. But they don't. They are first and foremost people of fear. Jesus reminds them of that, with words that we might call a dig.

SECOND COMMENT ON THE TEXT: It isn't clear where the disciples are. They may be watching from behind trees. They may be crouching in the darkness, not sure what to do. Perhaps they are still hoping that Jesus will lash out, fight back, or somehow escape from this pressing danger. Perhaps he will call out a heavenly air force or whistle for a secret band of defenders who will burst out of the shadows and slaughter these people who seem so determined to crush him.

But Jesus makes no effort to resist. Instead of pulling out a secret weapon, he calls his impending arrest a fulfillment of the Scriptures.

For the disciples, this is the last straw. There is going to be no victory, it seems. Their master is becoming not a hero but a victim. He's a loser. Hope is gone. Scandalized and offended at what they perceive to be Jesus' betrayal of the cause, they flee. Through the darkness on this Passover night, they forsake the one they have followed.

And so, as the strong man laughs in glee and just as Jesus has predicted, the sheep are now scattered . . .

TEXT TO READ: MARK 14:51-52

FIRST COMMENT ON THE TEXT: Mark's drama is always full of surprises, and this little side story about a young man who runs off naked is one of those surprises that often baffles people. Its inclusion in the story is obviously deliberate on Mark's part. Mark finds it revealing in some way—and not just because the man runs off without clothes!

Scholars have come up with many interpretations. Some have thought that maybe the young man is Mark, the author of the Gospel. But there is no evidence for that in the text, and it's clear from historical documents that when early Christians, who were closer to the events, wrote about this passage, they never offered such an interpretation.

Others have wondered if the young man is an angel, perhaps the same young man who appears at the empty tomb at the end of the story. But why would an angel flee?

Others have wondered if the story is meant as reminder of the story of Joseph and Potiphar's wife, where Joseph pulls free of her grip and loses his garment before being falsely accused and sent to prison. But the logical parallel would be between Joseph and Jesus, not between Joseph and an unnamed young man who happens on the scene.

SECOND COMMENT ON THE TEXT: Other interpretations have been offered as well. But one perspective that makes some sense is to assume that this is another of Mark's reminders of the message of the Jewish prophets. Mark often includes small details or distinctive phrases as a way of evoking the words of the prophets, and maybe the significance of this scene for Mark is because of how it calls to mind a passage from the Jewish Scriptures.

If so, perhaps we should think of Amos 2, where the prophet talks about the coming day of the Lord, a time when the sins of the people will be brought to an end, especially the sins of the rich against the poor and the sins of the strong against the weak.

The prophet says that in that day, when God brings redemption, soldiers will be stripped of their strength, those who shoot bows will handle their weapons no more, and those who chase after the weak will ride horses no more. And in that day, those who think of themselves as so mighty—those who think of themselves as so courageous—will "flee away naked."

Amos 2 also talks about the righteous being sold for silver, which Mark may have understood as an echo of the facts surrounding Jesus' betrayal. In addition, Amos 2 talks about a situation in which certain people "drink the wine of the condemned," a comment that Mark may have seen as somehow reflecting the Passover wine which Jesus shared with his disciples, all of whom have now fled from him.

BACKGROUND TEXT TO READ: AMOS 2:5-8,14-16

FIRST COMMENT ON THE TEXT: If this is the passage that Mark has in mind as he tells us about the young man running off naked, then the young man needs to be one of those individuals that consider themselves high and mighty. It needs to be one of those individuals who has gotten rich off the poor. It needs to be someone who has been counted among the strong and the swift.

And there may be a clue about such things in the one other detail that Mark mentions. The outer garment that the young man leaves behind is a "linen cloth." In Jesus' day, common people wear garments made of wool. Only the wealthy, the powerful, and those high in status can afford a linen garment.

So the young man who runs off is someone who has money, who has land, who has wealth. Perhaps he is one of the rich elders, a rising star, who is awakened in the night and told that the long-awaited arrest is underway. Perhaps he hurries out to Gethsemane, hoping to catch a glimpse of Jesus' capture. Or perhaps he is one of the priests or scribes who orchestrate this whole affair and, awakened from his sleep, has hurriedly cast on an outer garment (without the usual undergarment) and hurried along to see if all goes according to plan.

SECOND COMMENT ON THE TEXT: Perhaps Mark means for us to imagine that in the darkness and tension of this night, the group with the swords and clubs suddenly spots this man in the shadows. They're alarmed, not knowing who he is. Someone lays hold on him, trying to find out what he is up to. The man panics. He isn't supposed to be a part of the arresting group. He has followed along only out of morbid curiosity.

Unsure what to do, he turns to run, and in so doing, he loses his expensive linen cloak. Wealth steals from wealth. Evil turns on itself. And he flees naked through the night, shamed and humiliated, thereby serving as a symbolic affirmation of Amos's vision concerning the coming day of the Lord.

THIRD COMMENT ON THE TEXT: If this interpretation is correct, then it is with an extra measure of irony that we will be told, near the end of the Gospel, that after Jesus is killed, a wealthy man named Joseph of Arimathea buys a piece of "fine linen" and wraps Jesus' naked body in it (Mark 15:46).

In other words, Mark seems to be telling us, when the kingdom of God comes, when the day of the Lord dawns, roles are reversed. The strong and the wealthy, those who think they have it all—they lose everything. Not just their linen garments. But their souls. And Jesus, the innocent victim on behalf of all innocent victims, Jesus, crushed and abused, nailed naked to a cross—he, the shamed one, is about to be wrapped in fine linen. For he hasn't lost his life. He's found it.

It may not yet look like it. But the big bully will be bound, says Mark. And all his plunder will be set free.

And so, as the young man flees naked at the close of this scene in Gethsemane, we're reminded that in the cosmic drama that is unfolding, honor becomes shame. And shame becomes honor.

The one who "couldn't hear a mumbling word," the one who is forsaken by his friends and betrayed with a kiss—that one will someday be acclaimed. Not just by a few faithful friends but by choirs of angels. The one who breaks free and follows, the one who throws off his cross, the one who forever keeps taking up those terrifying things that are thrown in his path so that he might march forward in God's new way—that one will suffer in silence no longer. Thousands of voices will be lifted, each knowing, beyond a shadow of a doubt, that we can indeed take up beds and walk, for as an old spiritual says, there truly is "a God somewhere."